Master Your World

ISBN: 1-9357-3304-4
ISBN-13: 9781935733041

Master Your World

10 Dog-Inspired Leadership Lessons to Improve Productivity, Profits, and Communication

Mary C. Kelly, PhD

Table of Contents

"If more leaders treated their staff in the manner that Mary recommends— providing clear objectives, appropriate corrective guidance, and a fair number of 'pats on the head'— the elusive quality of employee loyalty would become commonplace."

- John Alexander, Director of Strategic Accounts, National Restaurant Association, CHART Board Member, Council of Hotel and Restaurant Trainers

"Doggone great read on leadership from a proven expert! Read Master Your World and never bark at a staffer, colleague, or boss again."

- DonnaLyn Giegerich, MBA, CIC, RYT

"Mary Kelly makes learning so much fun! Her down-to-earth approach to mastering leadership is refreshingly different and extremely effective. I recommend Master Your World to all small business owners who want to improve their bottom line and productivity."

- Barbara Harris, CEO, Harris Group Realty, Inc.

"Ten great lessons! From not rewarding bad behavior to doing the right thing at the right time, these are practical, realistic principles to live and work by."

- Cass Mullane, Beyond The Budget

"Mary Kelly's latest book, Master Your World, gives the reader a personal, practical, and poignant perspective on problems that plague those in authority. Her impactful dog-training

anecdotes bring home valuable lessons that make a difference in a positive, meaningful, and long-lasting way."
- Cris Carter, attorney, speaker, author, Cris Carter Law

"Mary Kelly's common sense lessons will reap great rewards for the employee, the manager, and the organization."
- Claude Berube, author

"Should be mandatory, refresher reading for all senior military leadership."
- Steve Kelly, Lt.Col., U. S. Marine Corps (ret.)

"A brilliant and masterful way to blend humor with leadership advice. If you want to mix business with pleasure and joy, this is the book for you."
- Loretta Milo, co-founder, MTI

"Want more productivity? Read this leadership book!"
- Andrew Wooten, President and CEO, S.A.F.E.

"How often can you say you enjoy reading a book on business and management? Inspirational and informative come up a lot, but fun? In Master Your World, Dr. Kelly gave me a message that profoundly affected how I think of my role as a leader. I've already adjusted some of my methods and seen results."
- Pamela Potter, COO, Zugg Software

"A brilliant and funny read. This book is the essential must-have for any manager, regardless of experience, to make you reevaluate the manner in which you lead."

With her amazing insight into the heart of most managers, Dr. Kelly has a brilliant method of getting inside your comfort zone. If you have a team of people or only one person who reports to you, read Master Your World. It just might change your life as well as those reporting to you."

- Rayett Cooper, former U.S. Air Force Senior Airman

"What a pleasure to read this! SO useful, helpful, and wonderful. LOVE LOVE LOVE it!"

- Cindy Bauschpies

"Mary Kelly has done it again, but not unsurprisingly. She has taken a unique, creative approach to write on a subject—leadership—about which she is an expert."

- The Honorable Allen Clark, author *Wounded Soldier, Healing Warrior*

"Mary Kelly has a wonderful way of translating the concepts of working with Man's Best Friend into navigating today's chaotic business environment. She incorporates her personal style into the pages of Master Your World to provide wonderful, humorous insights that can help anyone become better at what they do and how they do it."

- Vicki Harrison, Managing Partner, Optimization Partners, LLC

"An amazing and pleasing dose of reality on working with people. This book is a survival kit for leaders."

- Carolyn Betts, author, *A Special Kind of Normal*

Preface

This book is different.

There are thousands of books on the market about how to lead people. Some classics have been around for hundreds of years. But the problems facing managers and leaders today call for a different approach.

"The work ethic seems to have gone out the window."

"I can't get my new workers to get along with my senior people."

"No one seems to care anymore about what we do here."

"Generation X and Y don't talk to each other."

Sound familiar? These and other complaints reflect real problems, and they manifest themselves in lost productivity, employee frustration, diminished communication, and slow or mixed responses to customers.

What is a manager or supervisor to do?

Master Your World: 10 Dog-Inspired Leadership Lessons to Improve Profits, Productivity, and Communications demonstrates a systematic approach that works with people from diverse backgrounds, of all ages, at all levels of the organization, and, of course, with all dog breeds.

I admit it. Talking about my dogs is my way of tempting you to pick up this book. No, it's not about training badly behaved dogs, nor is it filled with fluffy, feel-good sentiments. It is about practical, sensible strategies for understanding people and getting the best from them. This book is not nearly as furry as it sounds.

As an experienced, practicing economist who spent more than twenty-one years in the U.S. Navy as an active duty officer, I'm accustomed to working with people from a wide variety of backgrounds. Working with people is both a privilege and a responsibility. I genuinely want to make the workplace better, improve processes, reduce unnecessary paperwork, and help people enjoy their work. I have learned something valuable from every person I have worked with.

This book reflects personal experiences and tried-and-true techniques for getting the behaviors and performance you want from the people you work and live with, and, yes, even with the canines in your life. It has been assembled for new managers, experienced supervisors, and team leaders who are looking to improve their workplaces as well as parents and community leaders seeking fresh ways to deal with challenges. If you come away with some useful dog training tips, that's an added bonus.

This book includes ten principles or lessons about eliciting the right actions from the people around you. Scenarios to positively affect interaction outcomes, including techniques that worked and approaches that didn't, are described in realistic terms—cued by lessons my dogs taught me. It also covers how to work with difficult personalities, how to manage your boss, how to transform poor performers, and how to reward employees in meaningful ways. For example, Lesson One deals with the basic training principle—Reward Good Behavior—and leads into Lesson Two—Don't Reward Bad Behavior. Lesson Three might be the most difficult: Being Consistent. The seven lessons that follow get more specific with actual "how to" details to implement changes and achieve the desired results.

It is my hope that this is a leadership book that will hold your interest and add value to the many facets of your life. I hope you put your paw prints all over it. Good luck mastering your world.

Mary C. Kelly
2011

Acknowledgments

My years of training people, dogs, and horses (I can't speak for training cats, but I'm not sure anyone else can, either) and the many people who spent hours, days, and months teaching and training me taught me how to get others to respond to what I was asking them to do. I'm passionate about sharing the leadership lessons that I've learned with other aspiring leaders who influence people on a daily basis.

Any credit for learning and teaching these principles goes first to my charismatic family for providing me with the basic foundations. My parents started and grew a fabulous business while raising four fiercely independent, Type-A, in-charge people. My brothers and sister and I all joined the military, and today we are fortunate to enjoy happy lives. My parents taught us to be generous with ourselves, share what we have, and work for the betterment of others. No small feat.

Throughout my military career, I worked with some of the most amazing people on the planet. The military people I know are hard-working, dedicated, and intensely focused on doing the right things. To the people I worked with, I thank you for your guidance and direction, for allowing me to learn and being patient with me.

I am exceedingly grateful to my friends whose constant support, encouragement, and humor allow me to explore ideas and projects, such as writing this book. I feel lucky to have the best friends on the planet; every day I remain indebted to their support.

I give heartfelt thanks to my dog, Rudder's breeder and amazing trainer, Trudi Gold, and her husband, Milt King, for giving me the gift of Rudder Nohea, my first Portuguese water dog. Trudi and Milt taught me that "there is no 'sometimes' in a dog's life" (Lesson Three) as well as other valuable lessons that apply to both canines and people. They cheerfully supplied green bottles (Heineken) and popcorn on Sunday mornings, along with practical and philosophical advice. Indeed, Trudi inspired so many aspects of my life, I can't begin to list them all. She truly is the big sister I always wanted.

My National Speakers Association friends and colleagues have been of invaluable help in both my writing and speaking career. They have welcomed me with open arms and open hearts, and shared their knowledge and motivation with me.

Any mistakes, of course, are my own.

My terrific editor told me that some dog breeds, according to the Chicago Manual of Style, are capitalized because they refer to a proper name. Therefore, the capitalization of some dog breeds and non-capitalization of others should not be construed as my personal preference of some dogs over other dogs.

Finally, I owe huge gratitude to Randall Dawson, who was there when I needed him, and has been there ever since.

Introduction

On a glorious day in May in Dallas, Texas, the sun was shining, the sky was blue, and the birds were chirping. People filed into the church. About a third of the crowd was dressed in their best military dress uniforms. My sister and I stood in the back of the church in our wedding gowns, getting ready to begin our double wedding ceremony. Our plan was to walk down the aisle together with Dad between us. If he got too nervous, we joked, we'd put him on roller skates and just wheel him up the aisle.

As we put the final touches on our make-up and hair, giggling all the while, Dad remained in the parking lot with the two grooms, dispensing a little bit more than fatherly advice. With the trunk popped open and the Igloo cooler inside, the guys were enjoying a prenuptial beer.

I became aware of this when my groom slid in beside me at the altar. I sniffed. He laughed.

"Sweetheart?" I smiled.

"Yeah?" he replied.

"Why didn't you bring me one?"

Thus began our marital bliss.

I come from the kind of Irish Catholic family that believes one's sole purpose on this planet is to provide parents with perfect, beautiful, talented, and way-above-average grandchildren. My parents were gracious. They waited a full ten months after our wedding before starting the inquiring phone calls.

"Where's the baby?"

"B-baby?" I stammered.

We had no baby.

A year passed. Another year passed. Another year passed, and still no baby. So my husband and I did what couples of the 1990s did. We consulted experts. We read books and articles. We talked to people. We interviewed, and in turn, were interviewed. We spoke to numerous doctors. We were put on a waiting list. After two long, arduous years of waiting, we finally got her. Bright blue eyes, a big smile shining up at us beneath a shock of black curly hair...and a wagging tail.

A puppy.

The puppy's breeder and first trainer, Trudi, told us, "You're allowed to have this puppy under one condition—you must train her well." My response came across a bit defensively. "Trudi, I train people in the military all the time. I'm well equipped to handle a *puppy*."

Or so I thought. Training this puppy—we named her Rudder Nohea, meaning beautiful new direction—gave me the motivation and inspiration to teach through this book, *Master Your World*. From the day we first saw her, Rudder Nohea taught me about enthusiasm, focusing on the task at hand, guidance for success, the importance of proper training, and much more. Thanks to Rudder and her littermates, it is my hope that others can benefit from these experiences and techniques. They have been tested and proven effective through the filters of experience working with employees, managers, and aspiring leaders.

I have been teaching at the university level since 1993. I adore my older students and I admire them for returning to school. But I also love young people. I especially enjoy working with teenagers. I've learned to love everything that goes with being a nineteen-year-old—the Mohawks, the piercings, the tattoos, the drama—because they became our new recruits in the military. I've loved working with them every bit as much as I've loved working with my new puppy.

A lot of people dismiss these raw, untrained, and undisciplined teenagers who join the military. They roll their eyes and think, "Ugh. It's going to take two years of training before these recruits are as productive as we'd like." But I find training them fascinating, and here's why.

Think back to your years of going to school. How many teachers did you have who truly reached out and touched your life? How many? Historically, the average number of teachers who strongly influenced your life is only two. *Only two teachers influence a student's life in a positive, long-lasting, meaningful way.* Every semester I teach, and every time I get to train, it's a great privilege. Because if I'm good enough, I might be one of those two influential teachers. As Henry Adam's autobiography states, "A teacher affects eternity; he can never tell where his influence stops." That's how I feel about it too.

Sharing lessons learned through this book is another way to pass on what I've learned, and it is my sincere honor to do so.

I would also be especially honored if you shared your leadership experiences with me and other readers.

It is easy to do so by leaving your comments on my blog at http://ProductiveLeaders.com/blog. I would love your feedback on this book, and I personally respond to every email at Mary@ProductiveLeaders.com.

LESSON 1
REWARD GOOD BEHAVIOR

Why Training People Is Like Training Your Dog

Everything I learned about leadership and management I learned from my dog. Well, maybe not learned, but definitely reinforced and clarified.

Let me explain. I've been employed to manage people for more than twenty years. Most management is about getting people to do what you want them to do, at the right time, in the right place, with the right results. We all know this. We take great pains to hire people with the right skills, and then we set them working toward the intended goals and outcomes.

Presumably, employees know their jobs, are capable of doing their jobs, and understand their instructions. Yet sometimes they still fail to do what's expected of them. So if *people* can't follow my guidance and do what I want, how can I expect my dog to do what I want? How can I *possibly* expect my dog to understand, when so many people clearly do not?

But my dog, Rudder, does understand. And she consistently does what I ask her to do.

So I had to ask, "Am I doing a better job training my dog than training my employees? What am I doing with my dog that's working so well?"

Further reflection on canines and humans yielded three important yet often overlooked management behaviors. The first lesson is for management to provide rewards, positive affirmations, or treats when people do something well. The second is to *not* reward bad behavior. The third is to do both of these behaviors consistently and in a timely fashion.

Most managers who don't reward good behavior wonder why they don't get what they want out of employees (or clients, or customers, or their eleven-year-old child). They rely on a few dependable people—trusted team players who carry the workload for the whole team. When managers need to get an important job done, they assign the tasks to the best workers.

You've heard the expression "Get a good horse, ride it until it's dead, then get another good horse." In the work world, that means someone who's used as much and as often as possible before getting burned out and is replaced by another "good horse." Instead of rewarding good behavior, those dependable workers are actually punished by—you guessed it—more work.

As a manager or supervisor, do you frequently forget to thank workers for doing a good job? Do you ever write a note to show your appreciation? Do you have policies and systems in place to reward rather than overwork your top producers? Or do you "ride your good horses" without noticing that they're burned out?

᠗᠖

Who Gets Rewarded and How?

When you really need something done, do you assign it to Carol, the hardworking wonder employee, or Harvey, who is *supposed* to do the job but is so unreliable, you can't trust that he'll get it done?

The people doing the right thing often get punished by being assigned more work while, paradoxically, those who don't do their jobs as they should—and leave others to do it for them—get rewarded with fewer responsibilities and easier schedules.

Is that happening on your watch?

᠗᠖

Show You're Paying Attention

When your dog wanders after you at home, he or she is "following" you; you are the leader. This sets the tone for your relationship, and the dog learns to look to you constantly for guidance. Once the dog respects your authority, he or she will pay attention to what you do and quickly learn from you. You encourage this behavior by making a training game out of the dog's natural curiosity.

To persuade a dog to "follow" you, playfully squeak a toy from another room and cheerfully call the dog's name. This attracts the dog to you. Yes, you're fun, friendly, and approachable, but you're also the leader. When you are "found," verbally praise the dog and give him or her physical attention.

This is how the dog learns to pay attention to you—both when you are in the room and when you are not. You'll be able to successfully call a dog from another room or outside, but first you have to get his or her attention.

One of the first behaviors humans teach dogs is to encourage a dog to respond to an assigned name. For dogs to "know" their names, they have to understand that you want them to do something special whenever you say that certain word. Using their names in a cheerful and friendly manner teaches puppies that a name is important. Whenever you call that special name, have a treat ready. That way, the dog associates happy consequences with the name you call, and pays attention to it.

When dogs are appreciated with positive reinforcement (treats work well, but so do pats on the head and time with you), they will deliver the behavior you want.

Employees also deserve to know when they are doing well. Positive reinforcement from managers for workers who are doing good work is often sadly lacking. Don't take my word for it. Go ahead and ask people where you work these questions:

- Do you believe you get the recognition from management that you deserve?
- Are other hardworking people in the organization getting rewarded for their contributions?
- Do you feel appreciated enough for what you do and who you are at work?
- Do you feel appreciated enough at home?
- Do you feel *over* appreciated? (I can predict the answer: "Almost never.")

Good behavior at work, unfortunately, is rarely rewarded often enough or in appropriate ways. Most managers think that giving their employees a paycheck is reward enough. Many supervisors grudgingly provide only the required yearly feedback at the required time while repeating tired lines about how valued the employee is to the organization and exerting themselves only in being careful not to upset anyone. Most employees leave their performance review meetings feeling relieved, not motivated or encouraged. Irritating to employees, time consuming for the managers and the human resources department, performance reviews are more often considered a mandated time-wasting nuisance rather than the means for helpful feedback or a reward.

I once met a manager who told me that when he gave directions to his employees, it was their responsibility to do what he dictated. He made it clear they didn't have to like doing it; they just had to do it.

On a certain level, he is correct. If work was meant to always be fun, we'd call it a hobby. But he forgot a basic principle and law of nature: behavior dictates consequences. Stephen R. Covey sums it up this way in his book *The 8*th *Habit*: "The leadership challenge is to enable people to sense their individual innate worth and potential for greatness, and contribute their talents and passion—their voice—to accomplish the organization's highest priorities in a principled way."

Wouldn't the work environment improve if his people performed their tasks from a sense of purpose and understanding, not just order taking? If a treat were waiting at the end of a job done over and above what's necessary? Covey reminds us, garbage in, garbage out. Instead, frequently when people work hard and are dependable, they get tasked with doing more work without so much as a "Thank you, well done!" How motivated will these "good horses" be in the long run?

Money Isn't Everything

I think anything worth doing in the market system is generally worth doing for money. I'm a huge believer in the capitalist system, but merely earning money is not why most people stay at their jobs. How do we know this? The most commonly reported reason people leave their jobs is not the paycheck, not the working hours, not the work they do, and not the commute. People leave their jobs because of bad bosses. People quit because in some way or another, their manager or supervisor disappoints them.

Great employees perform their jobs with enthusiasm and dedication because of their passion for their particular type of work, for the company, the cause, and/or the people they work with. As a leader, it's important to understand and then acknowledge what intrinsically motivates your people, and to show genuine gratitude for their superb work.

How do employees know they're doing a good job unless we as managers let them know that:

- indeed they are doing what we want?
- their work is definitely appreciated?

A paycheck makes a point, but it is expected rather than special. Anyone putting in the minimum acceptable effort gets paid. "Treats" such as thank-you notes, time off, public acknowledgment, and cash or gift card rewards given soon after an event show employees that when they go above and beyond the expected, you do too.

After all, dogs get treats when they do something right. So should those you supervise and manage. After all, what in this world can be better than a treat, especially when someone has earned it?

Employee Reward Programs

In his book *Mojo: How to Get It, How to Keep It, How to Get It Back If You Lose It*, Marshall Goldsmith makes a point about the human condition that we as managers are all too familiar with. "Our default response in life is not to experience happiness. Our default response in life is not to experience meaning. Our default response in life is to experience inertia. In other words, our most common, everyday process—the thing we do more often than anything else—is continue to do what we're already doing."

The challenge is to encourage employees to go above and beyond voluntarily and with a positive attitude. That's where rewards come in.

An employee rewards program that makes a positive difference fulfills three criteria:

- First, the reward has to reward employees in a way *they* find meaningful.
- Second, the reward has to be hinged to a measurable action, a specific activity.
- Third—and this is where a lot of leaders and human-resource managers screw up—the reward can't come at the expense of others and build resentment.

Let's look at each of these individually:

Make employee rewards personal—Giving meaningful rewards does not mean spending resources on a plaque that the employee doesn't want. In most cases a plaque is seen as impersonal and generic, plainly a cop-out by management. Alternatively, a stock of gift cards to local restaurants, movie theaters, and sporting goods stores doesn't incur any greater expense. They are useful, transferable, and have the potential to generate excitement among peers for the opportunity to earn them.

What motivates one person won't necessarily motivate someone else—tickets to a boxing match wouldn't get me jazzed at all! I'd be happier with a donation in my name to the local humane society because that shows that the giver knows what's important to me. It would reward me in the way I would fully appreciate. Perfect!

How do you find out what would work for your employees? Ask them! Have a short meeting with an ice-breaking game in which you ask employees to write down their answers to the following questions:

1. What is your favorite kind of food? Do you have a favorite local restaurant?
2. Would you rather have a gift certificate for Walmart, Target, or Home Depot?
3. Given a choice, would you prefer movie tickets, Blockbuster coupons, or pizza coupons?
4. Where is your dream vacation? Where would you like to go and what would you like to see?

Then ask them to share one part of this with the group, and now you have a ready reference when you want to surprise them with something they care about.

In the dog world, if you offer one dog a treat for a trick, other dogs in the vicinity will be eager for their opportunity to earn the same. People react that way, too.

ᚪᚪᚪ

Rewards that Acknowledge Effort Make a Difference

To be effective, match the reward to the employee in a personal way. My dad says the same treat that works for him won't appeal to my dog. I respectfully disagree. Dad wants a beer and a burger and frankly, my dog would be happy with that, too. It's my job to notice these things.

Part of expecting and rewarding good behavior is recognizing that you, as a leader, must effectively convey to the people around you what desired behavior is. For example, let's say I want someone other than me to take out the trash. I'm perfectly capable of doing do it. I'm strong enough. I know where it goes in the garage. I just don't *want* to take out the trash. So I'm truly grateful when the love of my life takes it out. When he does, I might say, "Sweetheart, I want to thank you so much for doing that. Every single time I see you take out the trash what I hear is you saying, 'Baby, I love you,' and I *do* appreciate you each and every time."

So what do you think happens? He takes out the trash! Positive reinforcement works.

ᚪᚪᚪ

Reward specific actions—Consider this: If I just sit on the couch and feed treats to my dog instead of requiring her to come, sit, or heel, I've just taught her she doesn't have to do any of the right things to get a treat. If she just sits there and looks at me imploringly with those big doggy eyes, and I give in, in effect, I've taught her to beg. I have not taught her how to be productive.

Some employee rewards programs work that way, too. They reward longevity instead of pro-activity and initiative. When management rewards workers for actual, specific results, and not for just showing up, employees recognize what gets rewarded and, on some level, realize what behavior they should emulate to receive recognition. I suggest you pair rewards with a few personal words or a note specifying the action that earned the reward. For example, you could acknowledge a project that came in under budget or the many extra hours your employees put in to meet a tight deadline.

Avoid setting up resentments—Now imagine for a minute that I ask both of my dogs Dolly and Rudder to sit, but I only have one treat to offer. Is there ever a scenario where that will turn out well? This is where the third criteria comes in: *The reward can't come at the expense of others.* Consider any employee rewards programs at your current or previous company. Many don't commend employees for working together toward a common goal. Instead, they turn employee rewards into a competition.

Limited opportunity reward programs actually encourage sabotaging coworkers to make them look bad. If a key person performs head and shoulders above the others, the reward program may result in feelings of jealousy, disdain, and dislike—or even elicit bad behavior that sabotages others. Some employees resort to less-than-attractive means of getting noticed and promoted, such as withholding information from their peers. Others might deliberately provide wrong information, like misinforming others that a meeting starts at two o'clock when it started at noon, just so their coworker would miss it.

There's a serious downside to a competitive reward program for any loyal employee. Actively pitting peers against each other through these programs doesn't result in cooperation among people at similar tiers in an organization. If your team could function properly without a certain position, then it would be structured that way. Each member is in place to offer specific knowledge and ability, and therefore each should have the opportunity to be rewarded for contributing exceptional effort. Revising your model to allow rewarding every deserving employee will improve performance while enhancing loyalty.

Don't Make Change Complicated

There are many ways to change an employee incentive program. The simplest, and my personal favorite, is to redefine "performance appraisals." This solution is sensible rather than revolutionary, and it should easily find support in upper management.

Here's how I suggest you do this. Instead of taking a more traditional confrontational approach, sit down with employees and discuss their personal goals for events and tasks within the organization. Help them develop a plan that will enable them to reach greater success. Ask them to fill out their own feedback form and discuss it with you. You might offer suggestions on ways to improve or offer more training if they desire it. Ask them what areas they'd like to learn more about, and what they'd like to change about their current job. Even if you as a manager cannot affect that change, your employee will feel listened to instead of criticized.

It's the Thought That Counts

As a leader in the military, I couldn't always reward my subordinates with vacation time because of constraints such as rotating shift work or involvement in a war. Nor could I give them cash; we aren't a corporation that can offer cash bonuses. But I *could* write them thank-you notes.

In 1997, I took over the security department on Barbers Point Naval Air Station, Hawaii, where I became the military chief of police. (We call them security officers in the U.S. Navy, while the Marine Corps calls them the provost marshalls.) The person in the job before of me was fired (for good reason). I inherited 300 people and a department characterized by low morale, poor processes, sloppy follow–through, and abominable record keeping. (One positive point about perspective: when accepting a position that has low expectations, if you're not horrible, you're bound to do better than your predecessor.)

This department had an inventory system that wasn't working. For twenty or so years, no one had seriously evaluated or audited the process. The person in charge of inventory had spent a year under my predecessor, which meant he had little instruction and no oversight. My suggestions for change met with strong resistance. I had to firmly stress that they weren't *suggestions.* (This *was* the military, after all.) In my best explanatory voice, I clarified the rules regarding government property and inventory control. Although I made it clear that *we were doing this,* I still got a great deal of passive resistance. Why? Because people in this department had previously done things *their* way and didn't like to be told to do things *another* way.

After a full three months of pushing various changes, I finally saw improvement—not only by the person assigned to do the inventory, but in other areas, too. Why the change? Clear expectations, consistent follow–through, and genuine appreciation when we had progress moving in the right direction.

Every Friday before I went home, I sat at my desk and composed a thank-you note—one a week (I couldn't justify too many more). I never made a big deal about these notes. I simply tucked a tasteful note card on the recipient's desk under the calendar. On some frustrating Fridays, I had to think hard about who I'd choose to thank. Even then, I had to liberally edit my wording, as you can see from this example:

Dear Petty Officer Jones,

Thank you so much for showing up to work this week, mostly on time, in some semblance of a military uniform, and for not setting the building on fire.

On behalf of the organization, let me say I really appreciate your effort.

Respectfully,
Commander Kelly

I recall one Friday when I sat down and wrote this note to my inventory control leader:

Dear Petty Officer Lawrence,

I just want to let you know I understand that the last few months have been difficult for you. Change is hard. I see your efforts, and I want you to know I really appreciate what you are doing.

Thank you very much.

Respectfully,
Commander Kelly

The following Monday morning, Petty Officer Lawrence walked indignantly into my office, held up the note, and asked, "Is this a joke?" Surprised, I looked at him and said, "No. I really appreciate what you're doing. Look, change isn't easy. I thank you for all your work. We've made good progress, and I want you to know I appreciate that."

His glare softened slightly as he turned and walked out. I thought, "Well, that was a waste of a note card."

But after a month, that note was still on his desk.

Fast-forward to two years later. The base had closed, and both Petty Officer Lawrence and I had moved on to other jobs. I happened to walk through his new workspace on another base and guess what I saw sitting on his desk? My thank-you note! I was shocked, but mostly I felt humbled that my note still held meaning for Petty Officer Lawrence.

It's amazing what a well-timed thank-you note, perhaps with a $20 Starbucks card tucked inside, can accomplish. The reward doesn't have to be huge. It simply has to genuinely acknowledge honest effort.

৯৯৶

I must also add that this assignment was one of my absolute favorites. I had terrific bosses who let me do my job and supported me throughout the entire tour. I worked with other great department leaders who helped me by sharing their valuable information, advice, and friendship. It was truly a cooperative work environment, and I have the commanding officers and executive officers of that base to thank for this fantastic experience.

৯৯৶

Use Rewards to Foster Loyalty

Every organization has a *loyalty factor*. Loyalty can be strong or weak, but it has to go both ways. If you *want* loyalty from your people, you have to give loyalty to them. That means finding opportunities for them, advancing their careers, and making sure they are well equipped to perform their jobs in a superlative manner. Loyalty by management means mitigating the problems and taking responsibilities for employee mistakes. Loyalty gives employees credit for their work and makes them look good in the organization. Loyalty works up and down the hierarchical chain. Leaders who are loyal to their people tend to receive loyalty and commitment in return.

It is important for managers to foster and encourage loyalty among team members as well. Consider employees who try to rise to the top by climbing over the backs of others, like crabs trying to climb out of a bucket. When you see this behavior, make sure it stops right away. If the climbers achieve higher positions through underhanded behavior or other less than honorable means, they're basically frauds. Allowing such behavior doesn't only reflect badly on your leadership, it's just plain wrong.

Bosses cannot play favorites either. Here's another example. Let's say Meredith is named Employee of the Month—every single month. The boss fawns over her, calling her the greatest worker ever. She reinforces her image by flattering her boss in return. Is she doing anything wrong? Not necessarily. But although Meredith performs terrifically well in her job, her coworkers tire of hearing about her superhuman powers.

When it's time for the boss to name the Employee of the Year, who gets the nod and the bonus? Yep—Meredith. By now, what do the other employees *really* think of her? That language doesn't really belong in a professional book; let's just say, resentment. And what happens to morale? It goes down.

As a result, are the others going to eagerly help Meredith on a project when she needs it? No, they won't because they're eagerly waiting for her to take that fall. If she gets promoted, people don't want to work for her.

With an Employee of the Year type of rewards program, when someone wins, everyone else loses and loyalty can disappear.

৵৵৶

How to Kill Loyalty

I witnessed plenty of examples of competitive rewards leading to resentment in the military. Frequently in an aircraft squadron, the most common U.S. Navy rank is an O-3 lieutenant or captain if you're in the U.S. Air Force, U.S. Army, or Marine Corps. A typical squadron might have sixty lieutenants. If you're among them, these people are your peers, your roommates, and your friends. You hang out with them and rely on them to watch your back.

Here's the problem. In the military evaluation system, everyone gets ranked with a number from 1 (meaning the best) through 60 (meaning the worst). The rankings are supposed to be somewhat confidential because they are part of personnel files, but everyone knows their number, so others generally know what number you and your friends are assigned. If you're rated at 59, you don't feel good about your job and if your number is 60, you feel worse. So what do you do? You think, "I'm at the bottom of the barrel. Why try?" On the other end of the scale, if you're ranked at 1, you might slough it off somehow and feel embarrassed or sheepish for being ranked above your friends. Or what if your roommate is ranked number 2, and you are ranked 59?

Not surprising, this ranking system results in hard feelings. Even worse, it creates an atmosphere in which you're *competing* with the people you should be *cooperating* with the most—your coworkers who should be your most willing, trusted collaborators. The system actively discourages teamwork.

In your environment, make sure people are set up to be loyal to each other, help each other, and work together, not pitted against each other.

∽◈∾

Show Appreciation, Decrease Uncertainty

Weren't the early 1990s great for people in the investing and financial industry? You could list of bunch of companies, put that list on a wall, throw darts at it, buy stock in the companies the darts hit, and make money. Weren't we smart when the market went up and we made money? Sure! Yes, it's easy to be successful when being successful is easy.

But what happens in a recession? Everything becomes more difficult, as we learned from the 2008–2010 economic downturn. It eliminated jobs and businesses; people were forced to change occupations, and retirement accounts tumbled in value. Fear and uncertainty increased as competition for jobs got tougher.

In the financial industry, the leaders whose companies survived became better than those who led companies in the 1990s because surviving a recession takes more effort and better practices from bosses and employees. Everyone works harder. Some people view the economic challenges as an opportunity to innovate and work smarter.

So *especially* during difficult times, make sure employees and coworkers, family and friends know you appreciate them. In all situations, whether at work, at home, playing sports, or leading a scout pack, always remember to *praise effort and reward results.*

Rewarding the employee for extra effort and results leads to more of the behavior you want in the workplace. Ask employees what they want. Some employees may need more time off and would prefer that to a plaque or a pin. Others may opt for the gift card. Still others might want to attend a conference that would enhance their professional knowledge. You as a manager learn this by listening to your employees.

Like giving treats to dogs when they obey your commands, you get what you reward.

❧❦

Nine Ways to Show Appreciation

Here are nine ways you can show your employees they're appreciated:

1. Time off
2. Cash
3. Public acknowledgment
4. Small gifts
5. Increased human capital (provide more training opportunities)
6. Promotions
7. Celebrations
8. Thank-you notes
9. Food/treats

Not all these ideas are applicable, practicable, or viable for all companies, but they may prompt other ideas.

Plus you can always ask your people what would work for *them*; you can be sure they'll have ideas of their own.

1. Time off—Few employees strenuously object when they're told to take a Friday afternoon or a Monday off with pay. They like having extra time for themselves to run errands and enjoy the luxury of not rushing to the next appointment in their lives. Unexpected time off has an added benefit for the workplace because employees tend to use that time off to accomplish personal errands—errands that they might otherwise be thinking about at work. With extra time to cross those errands off their to-do lists, they focus better on their jobs.

2. Cash—Nothing says "I care" like a cash award from the boss. Cash travels well, keeps well, and allows recipients maximum flexibility to get what they want or need. People *like* extra money.

3. Public acknowledgment—You can publicly announce when people on your team have a significant achievement in their business lives. Give credit where credit is due in front of as many people as possible and in the right forum. While a cash award might be more appreciated, at least public acknowledgments show that management is aware of their efforts.

4. Small gifts—Receiving small, thoughtful items expresses appreciation, especially if you want to thank many people and cash is not an option. Coffee mugs, pens, $20 gift certificates to Walgreens, Starbucks coupons, or anything personalized can be presented artfully and tastefully.

5. Increased human capital—Find the time and resources for relevant, career-building training opportunities. Good managers look for ways to enhance the personal and professional development of their people. So get employees into training. Helping them raise their education goals increases their sense of worth, further develops their skills, and ultimately benefits the organization as well.

6. Promotions—Once employees gain the skills necessary to accept more responsibility, help them find opportunities for promotion within the organization. Look within your own organization for quality people, spend the resources necessary to increase their human capital, and promote them. You foster both loyalty and teamwork by taking an active interest in the career advancement of your people. When employees believe they can be promoted within your company, they're more likely to stay with you and work hard.

7. Celebrations—Take time to plan joyful events honoring retirements, promotions, or other important milestones. Team-based achievements are great excuses for having a potluck, barbecue, or golfing afternoon. Such activities provide a break from work and get people together to build team unity. A cautionary note: If social gatherings are poorly planned and badly implemented, your team-building effort can be construed by employees as "mandatory fun," which breeds resentment for wasting their off-duty time. Promise a fun time and deliver it. A poorly executed event is worse than no event at all.

8. *Thank-you notes*—Your mom taught you to write them, but you still probably don't write them often enough. You likely don't receive enough thank-you notes, either. In the rapid-response world of email, a thank-you card says you cared enough to spend time to actually pull out stationery and thoughtfully compose a few words of gratitude. A thank-you note tells your employee, "I appreciate what you're doing," and is mostly underused. If you're one of the few who occasionally picks up a pen and writes, "Thank you for the extra effort with a difficult customer today," you get to experience that rare circumstance in which you can make both an employee and your mom happy in one action.

9. *Food Treats*—Bring doughnuts. Or cookies. Or anything else that can be shared by the group. Stop on the way to work and get enough for everyone. Bringing treats tells employees you're thinking of them and that you care. Nothing seems quite as good in the morning as a still-warm doughnut and sugar all over your fingers. Once, I was at an all-day company brainstorming event that was fairly miserable for everyone involved. In the last session, the boss showed up with ice cream sandwiches, "drumsticks," and chocolate-covered bars. It was such a surprising bit of fun that everyone responded happily. You'd like it if someone did that for you right *now*, wouldn't you?

My dogs love treats in all forms. Just remember people do too!

This option does warrant a cautionary comment. With the rising numbers of people with food sensitivities, be sure to tailor your choices to the recipients. If you have people with food sensitivities on your team and you consistently bring treats they can't enjoy, you'll be sending the wrong message. Vary your choices now and then to show you noticed.

ॐ

Chew on this

What can you do to reward people in your life—your employees, family, friends, service providers—and show your sincere appreciation?

Note: This chapter is more than twice as long as any other in this book—and that's intentional!

Reminder—Reward good behavior

- Take every opportunity to reward desired behavior. People need reassurance, especially in tough times.
- Make your expectations extremely clear.
- Create meaningful employee rewards programs that meet these criteria:
    1. Give rewards for specific actions or behaviors you want to reinforce.
    2. Make sure the reward itself has meaning for the recipients.
    3. Select rewards that boost collaboration, not competition, and don't come at the expense of others.
- Always find ways to appreciate the efforts of others, especially in difficult times.

Remember—Behavior that's rewarded gets repeated!

LESSON 2
DON'T REWARD
BAD BEHAVIOR

Don't Hesitate to Correct Bad Behavior

You are no doubt familiar with those workers who get away with not pulling their fair share of the workload. They show up when they want to, never come through reliably, and aren't team players. And guess what? Sometimes they outrank you in your organization; sometimes they're your peers; sometimes they work for you or live with you.

When you see bad behavior, do you correct it? Some people do, but frequently bad behavior simply gets ignored.

Why do managers and leaders hesitate to correct bad behavior? A few possibilities:

- Fear of confrontation.
- Physically afraid of the other person.
- Desire to be liked.
- Fear of escalation and possible hostility.
- Hope (mistakenly) that bad behavior will magically stop.

Consider this: If you continue to allow Martha to show up late, not deliver on projects, and annoy customers, will she somehow perform better tomorrow? Without giving her feedback that alerts her to the poor performance, it's a totally unreasonable expectation.

And it certainly wouldn't be a reasonable expectation for dogs, either.

I grew up with Dobermans. Here's a point to consider regarding Dobermans, Rottweilers, pit bulls, and other large dogs that people think can be dangerous. People are afraid of them because they are large, have big teeth, and are often portrayed in movies as vicious attack dogs.

I have to confess I feel more afraid of an unknown Chihuahua than an unknown pit bull. Why? A Chihuahua lives most of its life in someone's purse. Every time it gets scared, barks incessantly, or shakes (which is all the time), the dog's owner ignores the bad behavior, picks the dog up, and pets it reassuringly, saying, "That's all right, little Foo-Foo," even when the dog bares its teeth and growls.

That's *not* okay behavior by the dog or by its owner. The owner is reinforcing the undesired behavior, and then is surprised when the dog does more of it. (I actually do like Chihuahuas. I don't want hate email from people with Chihuahuas.) But my point is this: a Chihuahua's bad behavior gets reinforced more frequently than bad behavior by Dobermans, pit bulls, or Rottweilers, and therefore, the Chihuahua does more growling, snapping, and barking. Why? Because that's the behavior that gets rewarded.

How Bad Behavior Gets Reinforced

Does this happen often? Does it happen in real life? Let's say your little Chihuahua barks at a delivery man. Instead of putting the dog into a sit and making her calm down before you open the door, you take the easy route. You pick up the barking offender, thus giving her *positive* attention while ignoring and reinforcing her bad behavior. This is especially common for owners of small cuddly dogs. Why? You guessed it. It's harder to pick up and quiet a full-grown barking bullmastiff. Plus, little dogs are just so darn cute. As a result, you have increased your level of stress when dealing with the dog and when the dog deals with others.

Training dogs well makes life safer for kids and friends, and the dogs are more reliable and pleasant to be around. You want your dog to be regarded as trustworthy anywhere and with anyone. Isn't that what you want from employees or others you live and work with, too?

In your leadership role at work, ignoring or overlooking bad behavior hurts everyone. Your silence, in effect, condones (and therefore reinforces) the behavior you don't want.

ॐॐ

Her Majesty at the Post Office

One day, I went to a post office in Annapolis, Maryland, to mail a small parcel. I stood second in line with seven people behind me. The post office staff accommodated the customers efficiently, and the line moved quickly.

Suddenly a woman barged through the doors and strode directly to the front of the line. I looked around and didn't see Her Majesty's royal entourage, so I leaned toward her, pointed, and with my best, encouraging smile quietly said, "The back of the line is over there." I pretended she didn't know better or, perhaps, it was her first time in a post office. (It wasn't.)

The woman dismissively replied, "Oh, I just have a few things," then looked away. People in the line behind me shifted uncomfortably, watched the exchange with attentive interest, but no one said anything.

Again with a winsome smile, I took a step forward and said more firmly, "Oh, I assure you, the rest of us just have a few things, too. The back of the line is over there." I pointed to the end of the line.

Yet this woman still insisted. "But I *never* wait in line."

With similar persistence and still smiling, I cheerfully announced, "Then this is your lucky day!" I took a step closer to her and stretched out my arm and pointed like Moses with a staff, readying to part the Red Sea. "The back of the line," I enunciated my words slowly and carefully, "*is over there.*"

Her Majesty trudged to the end of the line.

Now, if she had said, "I have a baby in the car," or "I've got an emergency," or "My mother is in the hospital," I'd have taken her packages and mailed them myself. But I saw the postal clerks at their stations quietly snicker. Apparently this woman behaved this way all the time and *nobody did anything to stop her.*

Why? To avoid conflict. People decide rude behavior like this is not enough to create a fuss; it's "no big deal." They roll their eyes, accepting that the rude people will not change. But by tacitly condoning Her Majesty's bad behavior, they reward it. It's no surprise she continued to expect the royal treatment at the expense of others.

কৈক

Correcting Is Not Criticizing

Be clear on this. As a leader, correcting workers who are not doing their jobs properly doesn't equal criticism. In fact, developmental feedback from leaders encourages someone to be a better employee or a better manager. Great leaders let others know what behavior is desirable. Remember, if you don't correct your Doberman or your pit bull or your Rottweiler, your dog will never know what behavior you expect. It's not your dog's fault when it misbehaves; the fault is *yours* for not providing clear expectations, necessary training, and helpful feedback.

Apply that principle to poorly performing employees. If you haven't taken corrective steps to improve their performance, it's not *their* fault if they don't know what needs to change. Take positive, clear, and timely steps to explain what they're doing right, where they need to improve, and how they can achieve that improvement.

Allowing problematic behavior can have a negative influence on others. When you don't curb bad behavior in the workplace, you send this clear message to your employees: Don't strive for excellence. If Fred and Wanda continue to get the same employee appraisals as everyone else while putting in a third less effort, why should other employees work so hard? No incentive.

Both outstanding and poor employees deserve to know when they're doing well as well as when they're not. Just like expecting your dog to stop barking at strangers without giving feedback is unreasonable, you can't expect bad performance to improve if you don't address its underlying problem. It is part of helping your employees develop and grow.

My dog trainer, Trudi, would say rewarding good behavior while not allowing bad behavior leads to more of the same. The key is to acknowledge good behavior and gently correct bad behavior—every time.

"The Same" Isn't Always Fair

Treating people "the same" is not necessarily being fair. If you treat your son the same way you treat your daughter, you still may not be acting fairly. Why? Because children interpret actions and situations differently—just as adults do. For example, with your son, you might need to be firmer and more direct than with your daughter, who might require you to use more words to nicely explain why you want her to do something.

Adults, like children, interpret communications differently. For example, I don't react well to someone yelling at me. (I discovered few people do.) But I've had screamer bosses who started yelling from their offices and continued their rants until they were pacified.

If you yell at me to correct my bad behavior, I'll shut down, mentally call you an idiot, and probably ignore everything you say. Alternatively, if you gently and kindly point out that I was a schmuck and goofed, I'll dwell on that, internalize it, and make up for it a hundred times over. Yelling may work for some people, but not for me.

Learn to be extremely specific in tailoring requests to others. If I say, "Bill, I need your help on this project,"

Bill says, "Got it. Whatever you need. Give me the to-do list." With Wally, though, I might have to give him more detail to gain his buy-in. I'd say, "Wally, I need the following sixteen things accomplished, and I need them by Friday. Otherwise, funding for this program will be gone, we'll have to lay off three project managers, and our world will end. So I *really* need you to do this. Will you help me?" Wally needs details and consequences before he agrees to make this project his own.

I can just hear you thinking, "I will not pander to a prima donna employee." It's not pandering. It's using your extensive management training to understand your employees as individual people and putting forth a minimum effort to encourage them to put forth maximum effort. No, this is definitely not pandering. This is management, which means managing your most important resource, your people, in the way that allows them to maximize their potential. This also means educating them when they make mistakes, being patient with them as they learn, and making sure they understand your expectations. And then rewarding them when they get it right.

∂⊸⊷

Cop on the Corner

I recently moved into a new neighborhood and was out walking my dogs with one of my new neighbors. While we were chatting, a truckload of teenagers sped past. With a spray of dust the truck turned around and came charging back toward us.

"Will you do me a favor and hold my dogs for me for a moment please?" I asked as I gave my new neighbor my two dog leashes.

"What are you going to do?" he asked. "Oh," I said, "I just thought I'd introduce myself to these young people." My new neighbor didn't think this was a good idea. He mumbled something about the fact that I might get shot.

I stood in the middle of the road and authoritatively put my hand out like I was a school crossing guard. The truck stopped. I approached the driver side window, smiling. "How are all of you tonight?" I asked in a neighbor-like fashion. They replied with the expected head nods and grunts.

"I am very glad to meet you," I continued, "I am just meeting all of my neighbors. I just thought you might be interested to know that we have a cop who lives on this corner. Have a great night! Drive safely," I added cheerfully. The young occupants of the truck actually thanked me and drove off at fifteen miles an hour.

You don't have to act like a jerk in order to correct undesired behavior.

࿇

Flying with a Jerk

Imagine a crowded plane with no seat assignments. Now picture a very tall, broad-shouldered young man seating himself in the first row of the plane—the bulkhead seat, which has no seat in front of it.

The flight is completely full and this young man, who apparently is no novice plane passenger, lets his bag rest comfortably at his feet—a big no-no. Unless you have never been on a plane, you know that tray tables need to be stowed, seat backs must be in the upright position, and all carry-ons must be placed under the seat in front of you or in an overhead bin.

This large young man, having no seat in front of him, might have faced a dilemma. But no—when the flight attendant came to ask him to store his bag, our young man actually *flirted* with the attendant and requested that *he* find a place for his bag.

The flight attendant, rather than objecting to the rudeness of his flirtatious behavior or the effect of his request on other passengers, grabbed the bag and put it *under* the young man's seat. This intruded on the passenger behind our boorish protagonist, invading *the second passenger's* foot space for the next two hours. The large young man with the carry-on was rewarded with plenty of legroom. Indeed, this (obnoxious) creature placed his feet on the bulkhead in front of him and went to sleep. If our hero had not fallen asleep, I suspect the flight attendant might have provided him with a complimentary drink, so bold was his pandering.

This was a clear violation of basic dog training—that is, good behavior should be rewarded and bad behavior should not. Three people were affected by the interaction. The discourteous young man got exactly what he wanted by being rude and flirtatious; the flight attendant enjoyed the extra attention, and the man who did nothing wrong was penalized by having his legroom taken away.

Once you become aware of the first two lessons, you will see bad behavior rewarded all the time. It gets frustrating. Take heart, though. Sometimes what we see on the outside is not the full story. Wouldn't it have been funny if the man who ended up short on legroom was actually our hero's new, unrecognized CEO or another such coincidence? How do you imagine the *rest* of his day would go then?

Six Steps to Change Bad Behavior

Because as a society we shy away from conflict, there will never be enough training in diffusing bad behavior effectively. Here are some guidelines for addressing bad behavior I have found effective:

1. Make sure the behavior exhibited is what is truly going on with that person. Sometimes people have extenuating circumstances that cause them to behave out of character. We may not see this at first glance. For example, the person speeding down the highway may be transporting a seriously injured child. Or the frazzled woman with sixteen items in the express lane marked "fifteen items" may have her cancer-ridden mother waiting in the car.

2. Separate the behavior from the person. Good people sometimes don't behave the way they should. Once you separate the undesired behavior from the person, it takes the emotional component out of your reaction. This lets you objectively assess the *situation*, not the person, and determine the best course of action.

3. Address the undesired behavior immediately. It is best to correct in private; however, if you must do so in front of other people, make doubly sure that your

words, your body language, and your intent is conveyed as being helpful instead of confrontational.

4. Your comments should be directed toward altering the behavior. Many people mistakenly believe that corrections involve anger, confrontation, and a defensive reply. If you approach the other person with the intent of helping them, your actions can be perceived as being truly helpful.

5. Once you decide to correct bad behavior, and you know you're right, stand your ground. Don't let the other person bully you into retreat.

6. Work toward mutual victory. If my approach is to truly be helpful, both parties should win as a result of the changed behavior. More than that, I want the other person to feel empowered and victorious through gaining understanding or approval.

For example, say I had a New Year's Eve party. One of my friends showed up with a toddler who ran to my dog and grabbed her with both hands, screaming at her. What should I do to get the toddler and my dog to play nicely together?

I follow these six steps and check them as I do them:

- I recognize it as undesired behavior. *Check.*
- I notice that the child does *not* know what to do. *Check.*
- I don't criticize the child; I separate the behavior from the person. *Check*
- I want to help the toddler play with my dog so I am not angry. *Check.*

- I immediately show the child how to nicely pet a dog. I introduce her to the dog using the dog's name. I tell her that the dog likes her "inside" voice best, and the dog particularly likes to be patted gently on her back. I encourage the child to use animal-friendly gestures and sounds around the dog. The child's behavior changes. *Check*

- The toddler smiles and shouts with glee, "Mommy the dog likes me!" And everyone feels victorious. *Check.*

Chew on this

What can you change immediately to stop tolerating bad behavior or hesitating to deal with it?

Reminders—How not to reward bad behavior
- Don't condone bad behavior; ignoring it is condoning it.
- Help people develop by giving appropriate and timely feedback.
- Make the effort (as a leader, a parent, a pet owner) to correct undesirable behavior.
- Refuse to pay the price for not correcting employee behavior; if you don't tell employees they're not doing something right, you're actually hurting them by allowing them to become useless.
- Don't confuse correcting with criticizing.
- Tailor your communication differently to different people to get a better response.
- Rely on the six steps to change behavior.

Remember—Behavior that's tolerated gets repeated!

LESSON 3
BE CONSISTENT

Consequences from a Puppy's Perspective

For puppies, learning who's boss begins at birth. The biggest and strongest appear to get to the food first, but if that were consistently true, the runts would die from malnutrition and we know that doesn't always happen. The little guys figure out how to wiggle themselves into tiny spaces to get an advantage over the others. They have to be clever.

Dog moms also ensure that their littlest ones get fed. They'll move a pup from one location to another during feeding to make sure every pup gets a turn.

For puppies, mm is the boss. She teaches them to keep their sleeping area clean, washes them off, and brings wandering ones back into the fold.

She also tells them how to get along with others. If one pup is too rambunctious, mom provides a gentle correction—like a low noise or a slow push. When the pup is downright obnoxious, Mom either puts her mouth over his snout to exhibit dominance or gives a little growl, showing her teeth in warning. If the pup tests its limits with a nip, she nips back. Alert and attentive, dog moms provide immediate corrective action.

Puppies learn their best socialization skills with their baby teeth. Sharp doggy teeth can puncture soft and squishy objects, such as human skin. And like human babies, puppies explore the world with their mouths. When teeth are coming in, biting into things just feels good. The best way to teach a pup not to bite inappropriate objects (such as human hands) is to keep the puppy with its litter mates until they are seven to eight weeks old. Why? When a puppy bites a brother or sister, a retaliatory bite follows. Bites hurt and consequences are immediate and appropriate.

So at eight weeks old, a pup knows these three important lessons about coexisting in the litter:

- Respect the boss.
- Adapt around others.
- Actions have consequences.

Let's apply these principles to the workplace.

Respect the boss—In the dog world, the mom (or you, as pack leader) is the giver of order and discipline, the one who provides security and meals. Providing these essentials with consistency is how a pup's mom commands respect.

As a manager, you're the giver of all good things, but if your employees observe you behaving erratically and perceive that your presence has little value, they learn to discount your corrections and you lose respect.

Consider what bosses do to cause people to discount their authority and lose respect for them. They might:

- Implement meaningless rules.
- Easily lose their tempers over small irritations.
- Play favorites with employees.
- Create needless, inefficient work systems.
- Focus on small bureaucratic details instead of the big picture.
- Let ego get in the way of good decision-making.
- Ignore input from employees.
- Hoard relevant information, leaving employees in the dark.

In the work world, as in the dog world, consistency is key. Its absence fosters uncertainty, confusion, and disdain, leading to disgruntled employees and an expensive, high turnover rate. So like a puppy's mom, be consistent in your reaction and discipline so that your leadership is valued and respected.

Adapt around others—Puppies develop skills to get along with others and so do employees. Some might be bigger, stronger, or faster than the rest, yet those less gifted or a little slower find ways to "wiggle their way in" like the runt in the litter.

As a manager, you have to be aware of what's happening and be persistent in your efforts to lead well. After all, managing is all about getting people to do what you want to support your organization's mission and goals. In today's diverse workplaces, that means adapting your style and approach to what works best for each employee. You take into account cultural, geographical, religious, gender, and demographic factors and harness their differences and talents to contribute to your team.

This calls for flexibility, knowledge, patience, and appreciation for the strengths of each worker.

Show that actions have consequences—Behaving badly can hurt on many levels. Puppies learn that if they bite, they get bitten in return, and quickly figure out they shouldn't bite. (I'm not saying employees should bite their cubicle neighbors; that would be considered rude, and human resources personnel would have fits.) Put mechanisms in place to make sure employees who exhibit inappropriate behavior in the workplace get corrected—quickly and consistently. Canines know this and so should leaders.

There is No Sometimes in a Dog's Life

My dog's breeder and trainer, Trudi, has a mantra: "There is no 'sometimes' in a dog's life." That's great advice for dog owners—and for leaders, too!

Let's say you just got a brand new, completely adorable bull mastiff puppy weighing in at only ten pounds. You cuddle with him because, really, is there anything cuter than a puppy? (You might be thinking, "Yes. My child." I understand. But I'm sticking with the cute puppy example for the purposes of this book.)

So you pet and coo and cuddle with your puppy on the couch. He gets comfortable playing on your couch. The couch becomes your special place to hang out together.

Ten months later, your puppy weighs 180 pounds. One day, Aunt Sadie, who is eighty-seven years old, comes to the house and sits on your couch. The bull mastiff, with its jowly, drooling face, jumps on the couch and plops his face in her lap, expecting to be cuddled, right? That's what you taught him! And in the process, Aunt Sadie gets knocked over the back of the couch.

So what do you do? You yell at your dog!

Sure, his behavior was okay when he was younger, but now that he weighs 180 pounds, you've suddenly changed the rules—not yesterday but *today* when Aunt Sadie arrived. That's simply not fair. Dogs are not equipped to change expectations on short notice, and frankly most employees won't handle it that well, either. That's what we mean by "there is no *sometimes* in a dog's life."

As a leader, what do you do when you realize you have allowed people to take the wrong actions? You fix the situation. If you let undesired behavior continue and then try to correct it several months later, you essentially let the dog drool on Aunt Sadie on the couch. There should be no "sometimes" in how you treat employees, either. Just remember that changing expectations is likely to take some time and you, as manager, must consistently reinforce the new pattern.

Why Consistency Must Prevail

Employees need and deserve the same consistent direction as puppies. Yes, you can make policy changes; just be clear about what changes you want and what they can expect. But you have to be consistent in your communications—*always*. Remember, there is no *sometimes*.

Let's say Sam has been coming to work twenty minutes late for a full month. When should his boss have mentioned this to him, now or a month ago? After letting this behavior slip for a month, the boss finally tells Sam he needs to show up on time, but nothing changes. Not a surprise; Sam has lost all respect for his boss's authority. Remember, I can tell the dog to stay off the couch, but if I don't make it stick, he'll continue to join me after a few minutes. Employees are likely to be more capable of self direction than the dog, but some will require accountability to get the message. It's your job to monitor the situation and make sure the change is happening. Discipline isn't a *sometimes* thing.

It is difficult to be consistent. Anyone who has ever raised children knows this. Being consistent is trying because we get tired, worn down. We mistakenly hope that the behavior will change on its own. We sometimes try to delegate the consistency to others, hoping against hope that they will be consistent in our stead. Unfortunately, it's part of our job, and an absolute requirement.

Communicate expectations with consistency— Look for ways to reward people when they do their jobs well and dutifully arrive on time (or whatever you think is important for employees carrying out their jobs successfully). If they don't, help them perform better by clearly communicating your expectations consistently. Now, if every time I did something well and my boss gave me a mocha latte (or a Starbucks gift certificate to get one), I'd be motivated. Inspired. Enthusiastic. Cheerful. Also caffeinated, but eager to do more work.

Chew on this

How can you change your "sometimes" behavior to "always" behavior?

Are you being consistent in the actions you tolerate from employees and in the ways you reward them?

Reminders—How to lead consistently

- Respect the boss.
- Adapt around others.
- Show that actions have consequences.
- Communicate policy changes clearly.
- Be consistent: If an action was okay yesterday, it should be okay today.

Remember—Don't let "sometimes" behavior weaken your leadership.

LESSON 4

COMMUNICATE, COMMUNICATE, COMMUNICATE

Communicate the Way Others Learn

Communication is the number one way people get things done, yet it's the number one way to screw up the most. Here's the secret: You have to communicate the way others learn.

Dogs are extremely clear in the way they communicate with each other. They wag their tails quickly to indicate happiness. A slower wag with tails up can be the beginning of a warning. A straight or tucked tail and furtive glances can indicate fear. A growl is usually a warning, although some dog breeds are "talkers," meaning they exhibit noises that sound and look like growls but are actually playful. Other dogs know the difference, but people seldom do. Why? Because we have been taught that when a dog growls, it means the dog is unfriendly. However, what we see on the outside isn't always what's going on. Sometimes we need to gather more information to determine the reality of the situation.

Teaching in a New Way

My friend Janice is lucky enough to have boxers and at last count, she had eight boxers. She wound up getting Roger as a six-month-old puppy, because he was "hard to train." After three days, Janice realized what the problem was. Roger wasn't hard to train; at all. Roger was *deaf.* This was a whole new dimension in dog training for Janice, who'd never had a deaf dog, much less a deaf puppy. How do you call him to come to you? How do you teach him his name? Do you need to teach him his name if he can't hear it anyway? Janice realized that she had to teach Roger in a way he could learn.

Fortunately, she had help. The other dogs were already trained. Once Roger was part of the pack, it was easy. She whistled for the dogs, and all eight dogs came running to her. Roger cheerfully followed everyone else. The next time Janice whistled for the dogs, she also stomped on the floor twice, and after just a few times, Roger caught on that the two stomps meant "come." Janice also wanted Roger to sit on command. (All dogs know how to sit; it's just a matter of getting them to do it when you want them to do it. Sort of like teenagers.) Janice taught him to sit using hand signals. She gathered all of the dogs together, and said sit. Again, because everyone else was doing it, Roger followed. Janice got in front of Roger and simultaneously made a hand signal in front of his face. The other dogs taught him what behavior to perform. Janice just had to add a signal so that he understood that the behavior matched the signal.

A wonderful dog parent, Janice relied on her other dogs' abilities to train Roger in a way he could learn. People often remarked that they could not tell which dog was deaf, and they commended her for doing such a wonderful job training him. Janice modestly gave the compliments to her dogs. "I didn't train him," she'd say, "*they* did."

∂∞∾

I believe in communicating with people in the same way I do with dogs—that is, the way they understand. Scolding dogs hours after they scatter trash through the house reminds me of Gary Larson's Far Side cartoon that makes my point beautifully. The human says, "Bad dog, Ginger. Bad dog!" But what does Ginger hear? "Blah, blah, Ginger. Blah, blah."

That's true in the workplace, too. Communicating the way your boss or subordinate understands is crucial to achieving what you want. As the *Harvard Business Review* noted from John Maxwell's book, *Everyone Communicates, Few Connect*, the "number one criteria for advancement and promotion for professionals is an ability to communicate effectively."

How do you figure out the best method to communicate with other people? Many times they themselves don't realize which methods are most effective for them. You can try trial and error. Sometimes that is the only option. But it is also a more lengthy process.

It can help to give someone an opportunity to choose their own best communication method by offering them a choice of two. Use the same rationale that you might use on a six-year-old; you don't take the six-year-old to the restaurant and ask what he wants. When you have a child in the restaurant, you give him a choice of two. Would you like the chicken or would you like a hamburger?

This works in the workplace as well. Boss, would you like that answer by email or would you like me to call you? Boss, you asked for the demographics report. Would you like that in hard copy with a cover sheet and the summary page, or would you just like the raw statistics emailed to you? Boss, once I confirm your flight arrangements, would you like me to add that to your travel folder, would you like me to send it to your Blackberry, or both?

Most people can make a decision when given a choice of two options. They can actually choose a preference from three options. Given a choice between two options, some may spontaneously generate a third option they would prefer; by all means use that when practical. However, open-ended questions frequently leave both parties feeling confused. One person might respond, "Okay, I'll get that information to you." But if the person receiving the information just wanted a quick phone call, and you spent the afternoon compiling, tabulating, and summarizing the data, you have wasted your time and the organization's money. This is inefficient and frustrating.

How Communication is Changing

As it is with every relationship—canine or human—communication must be the cornerstone of everything. Remember, the onus of understanding always falls on the person communicating the message. Always, always, always!

Dogs let you know when they want something from you. Rudder and Dolly get dinner between 5 and 6 p.m. If there is no doggy dinner service by 5:30 p.m. Dolly does her "kangaroo" imitation—she gets into a sit-up position and paws at the air with both paws simultaneously. (It is, I admit, terribly cute, and not something she was taught by me. She learned this on her own.) Then she figured that when she did that, it might get my attention. (It did.) She figured if she got my attention, I might glance at the clock. (I did.) She figured that if I look at the clock, I might remember that it was doggy dinner time. (I did.) She figured that if she did it enough times, I would actually get up and feed the dogs dinner. (I do.) She trained me well.

She communicated to me in a way I understand. Do we always do that with our employees?

Good communication among people is comprised of listening, speaking, reading, and writing. Youngsters learn how to read and write English in elementary school and practice regularly through junior high and high school. But rarely do they get training in listening, speaking, or presentation skills unless they get involved in a speech competition or on a debate team.

These days, business communication is constantly changing across all sectors. Writing used to be formal and hierarchical. Most bosses wanted to see information only in written format. Now, thanks to the Internet and a youthful workforce, writing flows less formally, less hierarchically, and much faster, with messages meant to be read quickly. With instantaneous electronic communication, some people no longer have set business hours or even have to go into an office because they can access their work from their homes. And because of devices such as iPads and iPhones, they can read and reply to emails from anywhere at a moment's notice.

Although this trend may be unhealthy, electronic communications have changed expectations from others, too. I became enamored with a local printing company when I received a follow-up phone call for an email quote. Nothing unusual with that except that it all came at 7:45 on a Saturday night. The owner of the company (Allegra Printing in Colorado Springs, Colorado) wanted me to know I'd have the quote on Monday. I was impressed.

∽∘∾

How Do You Want Me to Inform You?

I once had a boss who got along poorly with his top managers. One day, I went into his office and said, "Boss, I want to do a great job for you, so I'm determined to make sure you're getting from me the information you want and the information you think is important. How do you want me to do that? Would you like it in writing? Would you like it in email? Would you like me to come and talk to you every morning? Would you like me to put a file on your desk?"

From that conversation, we worked out a system. Every morning, I went into his office and gave him a ninety-second verbal update and plan for the day. Then he gave me ninety seconds of his priorities and I left. At the end of the day, I gave him five bullet points summarizing the day's events. Whose conversation do you think I focused on in my bullets at the end of the day? *His* conversation. I was communicating in the way he learned best and about the subjects he cared most about. This setup made both our lives a lot easier.

உ௸

Hone Your Listening Skills

Communication must run both ways to be effective. For example, the first time Dolly did her dinner-time dance, I found it adorable, but it took quite a while for me to get her point. I needed to learn to "hear" what she was trying to say. Speech is a somewhat more precise tool for conveying meaning, but speaking cannot overcome failure to listen.

Honing your listening skills is of critical importance. To learn to listen more effectively, follow these suggestions:

- Give the speaker your full attention. People speak at the rate of about 150 words a minute while they think at the rate of approximately 500 words a minute. This leaves lots of time for your mind to wander. Be sure to concentrate on what they are saying.

- Focus, focus, focus on the person speaking. Don't get distracted by anything else that competes for your attention. Make others feel they're the most important people on the planet to you while they're talking directly to you.

- Express interest and vocalize encouragement in a conversation by saying things like, "That's interesting! Tell me more."
- Ask questions. "What do you think about this topic?" "What brought you to that conclusion?"
- Find the point. If people wander around without expressing their key message, help them rein it in. "What would you say is your main point?"
- Don't interrupt. When having a conversation, don't let anything—including your electronic gadgets—interrupt unless the building is on fire.
- Listen with your body. Your facial expressions, posture, position of your arms and legs, and the leaning of your body all signal to the listener if you're listening or not.
- Take notes. Jotting down ideas lets others know you're taking their communications seriously. It's helpful to ask permission first. "Do you mind if I jot down a few notes while we're talking to make sure I remember what you're saying?"

In *Everyone Communicates, Few Connect*, John Maxwell suggests, "At the close of a conversation, ask if there is anything you can do to help them and then follow through. Acts of servanthood have a resounding impact that lives longer than words." One of our most effective and powerful business skills is the ability to listen, *really listen* to others. We can help them with a recommendation and learn more about their business model, and we have just given someone a chance to talk about themselves. Because listening is an undervalued, under-taught skill, being an expert can give you the edge someone else may be missing. You'll not only be a better manager, but a better employee and friend.

Watch that Tail!

How often do you communicate with another person and believe you're successfully conveying the information you intended, only to get no response? John Maxwell gives us these interesting statistics:

- What we say accounts for only 7 percent of what is believed.
- The way we say it accounts for 38 percent.
- What others see accounts for 55 percent.

With dogs, closing the communications loop is easy. Wagging their tails fast shows they're happy; wagging them slowly can signal aggression. Similarly, people give nonverbal cues (such as nodding at what you say, but not really agreeing). You need to pay close attention if you don't want to misunderstand them.

Nonverbal communication is especially important when presenting information to a group of people. If you see yawning, diverted eyes, or doodling, it's clear that group is bored. If you see them crossing their arms and legs, they're resisting your message. Perhaps they're thinking, "We're not interested, we don't believe what is being said, and we don't want to hear it!"

The opposite occurs when you see people lean forward into a conversation. Their eyebrows rise, their eyes become animated, and they're listening with genuine interest.

How can you make sure people are hearing *and* understanding what you're saying? Read the nonverbal signals, get them involved, and ask questions. Find ways to double-check that what you said was heard—and watch for the human equivalent of tail-wagging.

ॐॐ

Do Something to Regain Their Interest

Being able to communicate well, both verbally and nonverbally, is the sign of an effective leader—and the cornerstone of every successful organization. Are you ever thrust into the situation of being required to address a large group without warning? Here are a few tips to help you keep your head above water:

- Keep your hands out of your pockets. Body language counts.
- Make an effort to deliberately look at individuals in the audience. Use eye contact.
- Unless your presentation comes as a complete surprise, practice! Out loud! More than once! The whole presentation! Every joke and every gesture needs to be practiced. Spontaneity is great on vacation, but not in a business presentation. Practice even more!
- Practice being loud enough to be heard. It is inevitable that the day you utterly depend on a sound system will be the day it breaks and the tech is out sick.
- Use voice inflection to keep the presentation interesting.
- If you are faced with yawns and bored bodies, do something quickly to shift the momen-

tum. Throw in a joke or change the subject slightly.
- Know your material and be prepared to answer questions.
- Have fun! When you love your audience, it makes the presentation easy and enjoyable!

࿇ೲ

If You're an Employee, Lead Your Boss

For some workers, supervisors, and managers, "leading their boss" proves to be the only way that things progress. It means you're supporting your boss in the best possible way, making sure your talents, strengths, and abilities directly support what the boss needs.

People can get frustrated with their bosses for various reasons. But if you learn to *manage* your boss through effective communication, you will have more control and influence over the situation. What's more, the relationship gets stronger and is often more successful.

Consider leading your boss in these ways:

- Communicate in the boss's style.
- Reassure your boss with information.
- Keep your boss informed and involved.
- Support your boss in meetings.
- Praise your boss to others.

Communicate in the boss's style—Get him or her to do what benefits you, your people, and your department by setting up an effective communication procedure, as my example showed. Another boss I had couldn't understand what I said when I sat in front of him and gave him information. Everything had to be written down for him because he needed time to digest the information before talking about it. So the solution was sending written reports and telling him *when* I would follow up in person.

Reassure your boss with information—I've found it helpful to give my bosses a short summation of events at the end of every day. By doing that, I also give them a security blanket so they don't have to wonder what's happening in my department. I answer their questions before they know what to ask. What's reassuring for them benefits everyone in my part of the organization because the top leaders know what my people are doing.

Keep your boss informed and involved—Some bosses only like to be involved in the happy parts—the jelly in the sandwich—not the difficult parts. Maybe they want to get involved only with awards and upbeat presentation letters while you take care of the not-so-nice parts. Keeping these bosses informed and involved in your successes will keep them happy with you and your people.

Some bosses like to know about problems, even the small ones. That's okay. Explain the problem and determine the solution. I liken this again to children. If they come home one day and tell you about a difficult situation, and then they convey the good decisions they made, it increases your trust and confidence in their ability to handle future events. The same is true at work. Some managers don't like to tell their bosses they're having problems because they think it makes them look bad. (Some bosses also don't want to hear about problems at all. Problems give them headaches.) Most bosses I know would rather know about the problems early so that they can react, if necessary.

Support your boss in meetings—This doesn't sound like a big deal, but bosses can feel unsure of themselves in public situations. I'm not suggesting giving big group hugs. You can simply agree with your boss in front of others by saying, "I think that's a great point. Maybe we can do *this* to better support *that*," or "Maybe *this* idea would be a good way to continue that idea." Show active attention and support. Leave any disagreements to be discussed in private. This does not mean that you need to become obsequious. It means that you publicly show teamwork to others.

Praise your boss to others—Tell other people about the good job your boss does. Consider it a bonus if your comments get back to him or her. Bosses don't always know how well they're doing; nothing is better than knowing their employees value them. Compliments mean most when a third party with no vested interest in the situation passes along your comments.

Chew on this

What styles of communication works best for the various people you work with?

How can you lead your boss in a way that can help your people as well?

Reminders—How you communicate makes a world of difference

- When you're listening to someone talk, that person deserves your full attention.
- Pay attention to nonverbal cues.
- Always communicate in the way others learn.
- "Lead" your bosses by supporting them, offering reassurance, providing information, and telling others what a great boss you have.

Remember—The onus of conveying the message and making sure the message is received always falls on the communicator.

LESSON 5
PLACE THE RIGHT PEOPLE IN THE RIGHT JOBS

What Characteristics Make You a Leader?

Have you ever taken your dog to a dog park? Have you ever seen dogs greet each other when they meet for the first time? They have an immediate way of determining which one of them is in charge. Many people think that the big dogs are always in charge. That is often not the case. It is all about personality.

Growing up, our family had Dobermans. One day Mom brought home an elderly Shih Tzu whose owner could not care for her any more. When Duchess, the 150-pound Doberman, went to play with Tinker, the 15-pound Shih Tzu, Tinker snarled and the Doberman actually dropped down on her back to signal submission. Tinker was clearly the alpha dog, even though she was one-tenth the Doberman's size and several years older. Tinker established authority right away, and Duchess, being a more amiable dog, succumbed to her new second place in the hierarchical doggy world.

This is one of the lessons I tell new teachers. You only get one chance to walk into your first class and make it clear that you are the alpha—that *you* are the one in charge, and students who challenge you in an inappropriate way will lose. If you don't establish your place at once, they will never accept it, and you'll experience disruptions and arguments all semester. The trick is, you have to know it in your own heart to make it stick.

How do you get to ownership of your leadership position? Think of a single event in your life or at work that made you a better leader. Contemplate for just a minute about that one single event.

I'll bet the memory you're thinking of had something to do with a tough situation. Just as heat tempers steel, solving huge problems makes us better leaders, especially during touchy, difficult situations. John Maxwell, in *The 21 Indispensable Qualities of a Leader*, gives excellent insights on the makings of a leader with these words: "Crisis doesn't necessarily make character, but it certainly does reveal it. Adversity is a crossroads that makes a person choose one of two paths: character or compromise. Every time a leader chooses character, he or she becomes stronger, even if that choice brings negative consequences."

If you have a moment of doubt about your leadership ability, just think back to that one event and recall your exceptional response. Once it becomes a habit, you'll lose your doubt.

How anyone responds in a crisis largely depends on natural ability, training, and previous experience. When teaching young men and women in the military, their leaders strive to instill and reinforce the values expected as well as the characteristics needed to make good decisions in an emergency. Because of the different environments, you'll find that the characteristics your friends use to describe you differ greatly from the characteristics used by those you work with closely, often under fire. Thinking well of and expecting the best from people will go far in encouraging them to deliver their best.

Isn't that one of the fundamental functions of leadership—to bring out the best in those we lead?

❧❧

What Characteristics Describe You?

From the following list of characteristics, select three that best describe what you contribute to your workplace.

Personable
Friendly
Sweet
Technically solid
Technologically advanced
Good researcher
Thorough
Attentive
Conscientious
Considerate
Cooperative
Patient
Lively
Brilliant
Active
Adventurous
Affable
Amiable
Capable

Ambitious
Ethical
Faithful
Happy
Polite
Impartial
Determined
Respectful
Logical
Loquacious
Excited
Concerned
Obliging
Careful
Charismatic
Meticulous
Cheerful
Computer-oriented
Encouraging
Energetic
Enthusiastic
Handy
Harmonious
Imaginative
Confident
Candid
Logical
Easygoing
Eloquent
Clever
Hopeful

Exacting
Mature
Joyful
Competent
Mission-oriented

ॐॐ

When I was military chief of police in Hawaii, I picked these three characteristics that described me: impartial, imaginative, and mission-oriented. I chose them because I believed these were good characteristics for my position. Limited resources, having to maximize my personnel, and fighting crime all fit into this role... or so I thought!

My boss, however, chose different characteristics for me in this job. He wanted me to be friendly, patient, and easygoing. Uh-oh. But once we talked through the situation, I changed my focus to align with his characteristics, and I'm grateful that we discussed his expectations. His clarification of how he perceived my job gave me guidance to properly convey his vision for our department. It also ensured that I fully developed those skills he believed would best benefit the people working on that base.

Find out what characteristics your boss expects you to have at work. You can initiate a dialogue by saying, "Boss, these are the characteristics I think I bring to the table, but they may not be what you want. What characteristics would you like me to focus on?" A statement like this sets up a valuable feedback discussion and tone for a good working relationship.

If you are the boss and you have employees you trust and respect, ask them what they need from you as their leader. Doing this fosters communication between you that builds trust and loyalty and leads to everyone's success.

For fun, start a similar discussion about desirable characteristics with your spouse or significant other. See how that goes—and how it differs from your workplace conversation! Here's an example. When my sweetie and I were at dinner, I whipped out the list of characteristics and asked him which ones he wanted me to display. He froze! "Is this a trick? Did you get this from one of those women's magazines?" I laughed and reassured him that I wanted to exemplify the characteristics *he* desired in a life partner. I admit, though, the characteristics he was looking for were *not* on this list.

Leaders leverage their people's strengths to help the organization stay competitive during difficult times. That means hiring great people and making an effort to develop them. How? By giving them an opportunity to tell you what they love to do. Then you're leveraging their strengths for the good of your organization.

Find the Right Person for the Right Job

Placing the right people in the right jobs for them requires leadership in action. In fact, matching people, talents, and skills with what you need is like dating. In many ways, it *is* dating. After all, you'll spend inordinate amounts of time with the people you hire, possibly more than you spend with your spouse, so make sure it's a strong working relationship.

I admire leaders who hired great people early in their careers and continued to find positions for them, even years later. After working with hundreds and thousands of people, I wanted to hire many of them later when I got my own company. And I did. That's the power of leveraging strengths.

❧❧

My Best "Date" at Work

The best "date" I ever had at work was with a gentleman named Dan Tom. Mr. Tom, a dedicated, astute former naval officer, knew my job better than I ever would. He had performed all the job functions in our organization and had risen through the ranks to boot, so he understood its political nuances, too.

The best part? Mr. Tom had my back. He made my priorities his priorities. We disagreed occasionally in private, but when we addressed our teams, we presented a united front.

It helped that we had similar responses to problems and reacted in similar ways. The issues that bothered Mr. Tom (union allegations, employees showing up late, unwarranted employee complaints) I was happy to handle. The issues that irritated me (reports, more reports, reporting statistics, error reports, and billet alignments) he dealt with beautifully. I was lucky to work with him. He was also funny, kind, and tough in the best possible way.

Dan was on permanent staff and therefore stayed with the organization after my military tour there was complete. Someone else in his position could have made my two years at the helm miserable by engaging in a power struggle or trying to usurp control. Instead, Dan taught me important leadership principles. He did his best to make the organization (and me) look good.

❧❧

Not all employees are created equally. Neither are dogs. A toy poodle is not a border collie. Sure, they're both dogs, but please don't ask the toy poodle to herd sheep. The toy poodle would attempt to herd sheep with its little heart in the right place, but in the end, the results wouldn't be satisfactory.

People, like dogs, have individual talents and abilities. The way managers assign tasks and motivate their employees needs to differ from one person to another.

That's why considering individual strengths and personalities is imperative when assigning tasks. You wouldn't ask an introverted person to initiate a cold-calling campaign, just like you wouldn't ask a toy poodle to herd sheep.

Play to Their Strengths

The hiring process is rather abrupt. You review résumés, you spend an hour with a few people, and then you hire someone for a job description written long ago and far away. It's expected that people will fit into these paper descriptions. Marcus Buckingham, in his books *The One Thing We Need to Know* and *First, Break All the Rules,* claims that most people aren't playing to their strengths at work. Instead, managers put "square pegs" into "round holes" and attempt to make them *become* the workers they want them to be.

This outdated and inefficient way of managing simply won't work. Buckingham asserts that all employees have core strengths, affinities for certain skills, and innate abilities. Such abilities allow them to excel in specialized roles that they find easy and enjoyable. Employees in jobs that directly correlate to their strengths are happier, more productive, and more apt to succeed.

Proper training helps employees combine their inherent strengths—the qualities they were hired for, we hope—with the goals of the organization and the needs and expectations of their specific position. This is particularly critical during a recession or economic downturn. Why? If people aren't fully trained to do their best, resources get wasted and opportunities lost. And what organization can afford to allot time for fixing problems caused by poorly trained people, recession or no recession?

Some employees and senior people resist going through a training program, claiming, "I already know how to do my job." But when you are in a leadership role, your idea of what's needed may be radically different from theirs. Training addresses these differences for the good of the organization.

Proper training combined with proper placement also puts the right employee in the right job. That's why it's critical to explore preferences, perceptions, and experience levels before committing your people to a training program. Do you really expect someone who has only worked the window in a fast-food restaurant to serve a banquet at the Ritz-Carlton without training? No, you don't. Certain employees may have great attitudes, but without training, they won't be as effective as you need them to be.

Today, I know certain aspects of running a business aren't among my personal strengths—like typing, filing, keeping my desk tidy, and formatting my e-newsletter. I *can* do these tasks, but I don't *like* doing them. In fact, I dread the idea of even starting these tasks.

Because I know this about myself, I pair up with people who handle the administrative nuts and bolts. Once I find them, I rely on them to keep me scheduled and on track. Not only that, but I tell my administrative people to give me direction. If I have to meet a deadline, they remind me. By relying on their talents, I'm able to keep my business running smoothly.

Buckingham wasn't the first person to encourage specialization. In 1776, Adam Smith wrote *An Inquiry into the Nature and Causes of the Wealth of Nations.* Smith said workers could be far more productive if they specialized, so clearly this idea isn't new in the twenty-first century. It's why people no longer change the oil in their cars themselves. Going to a specialized oil-change service provider is more efficient, less time-consuming, and far cleaner, too.

Reassuring Messages and Pats on the Head

My dogs like to have their ears rubbed and their coats petted. I love the way they respond, leaning into my hand to show they enjoy the attention. Yes, I know. Giving pats on the head won't fly in the workplace. But make sure people around you know that their continued efforts and the resulting superior performance deserve rewarding, too.

During the recent economic downturn, people who would otherwise not worry about job security—bank tellers, computer technicians, union autoworkers, restaurant chefs, even police officers—suddenly found their livelihood in peril. Without reassurance from their organizations that their jobs are secure, employees act like people who believe they're losing their jobs by default. Their productivity slides as their anxiety increases. They engage in rumors and speculate about the fate of the organization. These at-work conversations lead to worrisome, anxiety-filled talks at home as they waste countless hours wondering, "What if I lose my job, too?" "What if my income stops?" "What if I have to go on unemployment?"

Some managers wrongly surmise that if employees are concerned about job loss, they'll work harder. Not true. Most will polish their résumés, log into job-hunting websites, send out feelers to colleagues in other organizations, and write cover letters- and all while at work.

Under these circumstances, what do effective leaders do? Provide a human version of patting their employees on the head and give messages of reassurance. People understand that life offers few guarantees, but they also like to believe a work contract will be honored. Give them that feedback. Make sure they understand they are valued and watch their attitudes shift. They'll look forward to long-term planning and work hard toward common goals—if they feel reassured that they're needed.

Ask a dog. There can never be too many pats on the head!

Chew on this

How can you learn from crisis situations to become a stronger leader?

How can you best employ the talents and strengths of your people?

How can you use reassuring words to improve productivity?

Reminders—How to place the right people in the right positions

- Find out what characteristics your boss and your employees expect you to display in your job.
- Use strength-based modeling to put the right person in the right job.
- Make sure your employees know they're appreciated and secure in their jobs.
- Reward your employees' efforts and communicate their value to the organization, especially during tough economic times.

Remember—Your leadership success depends on helping others succeed.

LESSON 6
PROVIDE THE RIGHT TOOLS

The Right Direction

Right now, wherever you are, do you know where north is? Being on the Front Range of Colorado is great because when you're outside, you can simply stand with the Rocky Mountains on your left and look forward. That's north.

But what if you're in an environment that doesn't let you know what direction you're facing? Doing the right thing sometimes requires asking for directions. And often success depends on *whom* you ask.

One of my policies in a former position as chief of police was making sure employees knew when they should call for backup. They would work a situation as far as they could, then call for reinforcements, which often involved bringing in the right tools so that they could proceed in the right direction.

Start with These Three Tools

It doesn't matter whether you're eating at restaurant or buying a book or a house, you want three outcomes when purchasing a good or service:

- A great product.
- Pleasant interactions with personnel.
- Easy and clear procedures.

If you're ever at a loss knowing how to improve business, examine these three outcomes and execute them as consistently as possible.

To explain what I mean, let me share this example about buying food for my dogs.

My breeder encouraged me to feed my dogs well. If the truth is known, they eat healthier food than I do. Why? When I get hungry, I might pull out a bowl and enjoy frosted flakes for dinner with a glass of wine. But my dogs get the same balanced kibble they always get (unless Mommy happens to make them chicken and baked potatoes and broccoli).

I was delighted to find a local store that carries the healthy organic "happy" dog food, the kind movie stars probably feed their pampered canines, too. No preservatives, no additives, no corn, no gluten—you get the idea.

Imagine my dismay when the store stopped carrying my dogs' favorite brand of dog food. When I asked about it, they assured me they could order it for me by the case.

"No problem," I said. "How many bags in the case?"

"Four."

"Super!" I said, and we placed the order.

Forty-eight hours later, a store clerk named Steve called to say my case of dog food had arrived. Fabulous! When I arrived at the store, I found Steve and he took me to the back where he presented me with a case of the dog food I wanted. He then reminded me to tell the cashier about the ten percent discount on case items. I was pleased.

When it was my turn at the cashier, I said with a warm smile, "Steve in the back says you have a ten percent discount for cased items. Isn't that great?"

The cashier apologized, "Oh, I don't know how to do that. This is my first day." So he called Steve on the phone. Just then, the cashier at the other register said, "No, we don't do discounts on dog food. It's only for people items." (She's clearly a cat lover.)

My poor cashier was completely confused. He didn't know if he should take the items out of the case (which was taped shut for my convenience) to find a price. That's when the store manager came over and loftily barked directions. "Look, just scan the case, then multiply times four." The machine scanned for the *entire* case and suddenly the cost of my dog food totaled an unexpected several hundred dollars. I waited for them to discover the overcharge, but had to point it out myself. The manager realized her mistake, cleared the transaction, and told the cashier what the price should be—no case discount offered.

Now, all I wanted was dog food. Steve gave me terrific customer service. Although the cashier didn't know how to do what needed to be done, he cheerfully tried, and then followed procedure by calling for help. Perfect! Both he and Steve understood customer service and gave me:

- A great product.
- Pleasant interactions with personnel.
- Easy and clear procedure.

The store manager? Well, she didn't make the grade.

Even the Little Things Help

People need the right tools to do their jobs, both at work and at home. Frequently the right tool is training, but sometimes it's something stupid like purple paper clips, as I experienced when I lived in Hawaii.

There, the climate is sunny with high humidity. Metal objects rust quickly when the humidity is high. In my job, I was in charge of many, many file cabinets full of papers stapled together with metal staples that had rusted and made spots on those papers. AHA! I thought if I could use plastic-covered paper clips, I could prevent all those rust spots, which seemed to appear five minutes after I put a metal paper clip on a piece of paper. To solve this problem, I approached my boss and said, "Boss, I want to spend a dollar nineteen on plastic-coated paper clips."

"No," he replied. "We've always used the metal ones. No reason to change."

In trying to persuade him, I explained the economic reasons for making this simple change from metal clips to plastic. "I've got all these rusted folders of papers dating back to World War II. I have a rusted file cabinet and now it's rusting from the inside out. It's hot, it's humid, it's Hawaii, and we don't have air conditioning." I thought my persuasive skills made perfect sense.

"No," was his answer.

After work that day, I went to the office supply store and bought $1.19 worth of plastic-coated purple paper clips. For only $1.19, we realized exponential savings from not having to redo paperwork. It saved retyping countless papers for me and for future generations.

Which tools help you do your job better day to day? Do you like to use certain gadgets? I carry around yellow legal pads and good, cheap pens—the right tools for me. (When I travel, I also carry a technology bag with a GPS, my iPod, a video camera, a regular camera, and of course, my phone and laptop. I've also been known to include a tape recorder, adapters, microphone, and a business card scanner.)

How do you figure out what your employees need to do their jobs better? Ask them—and don't sweat about spending $1.19 for plastic paper clips if they're the right tool for the job.

Keep the Dogs Out of the Trash

My dogs, Rudder and Dolly, are clever. The older one, Rudder, has figured out how to open childproof cabinets, garage doors, and, of course, self-opening trash cans. You know—the trash cans with the motion sensor that makes the lid fly open? Rudder loves that one. Playing with it is like Christmas to her.

One day, Rudder somehow got access to the trash-can, tipped it over, and spread its treasures around the floor. That way, she could share them with Dolly. Together they delved into the eggshells, coffee grounds, crinkled-up toothpaste tubes, yogurt containers, and one whole date-expired blueberry pie. The pie, naturally, was a special find, and thus required delicate handling. The two dogs somehow managed to move the pie to a place that would provide ambiance and comfort for their doggy-dining pleasure. That place? My bed.

A blueberry pie with remnants of Cool Whip.

I wanted to be mad, but it's hard to scold two furry faces covered with blueberries.

"Did you do this?" I demanded of them, my voice firm.

The dogs exchanged a glance and then looked back at me. "Oh, no, Mom! Not us!" Wag! Wag! Wag!

The pie was a lesson for me—don't set the dogs up for failure. It was clearly my fault for not padlocking the trash cabinet, so I couldn't be angry with them. But this pie escapade reminded me I had to be a step ahead of them. A mere under-the-sink kitchen cabinet for the trash? Child's play. I installed a child-proof latch. That was child's play too. Rudder figured that out in about three days.

I resorted to taking out the trash every time I left the house. Inconvenient, yes, but not nearly as time-consuming as cleaning up blueberry pie in the bed. When I looked for a new place to live, one of the attractive features was a broom closet that had a tough-to-turn handle on a real, full sized door. Trash is now safe. More importantly, the dogs are now safe, and I don't have to worry about a mess. Their environment and the dogs are now set up for success.

Set Them Up for Success

For some bosses, setting up employees for failure happens all too often. One boss I had even enjoyed it. No matter what his people did, it wasn't right because he had withheld critical information they needed to successfully complete their projects. The downside of his practice was overly apparent:

- Work was always delivered late because last-minute adjustments had to be made to include the missing components.
- In his eyes, work was never completed correctly.
- People stopped working hard for him, knowing the job order would change at the last minute. Why do the work twice, they reasoned.
- People immediately responded with cynicism when he spoke.
- Production suffered, morale plummeted, and costs increased as people eventually fled his work environment.

People like to go to work and excel. If they can't, they get demoralized. They certainly don't like to be scolded for doing what they were trained to do, and for doing what they believe they should be doing. Results can be disastrous. By hoarding information and not giving employees necessary resources, that boss destroyed his department and his own career.

Employees need the right tools, information, and other resources to succeed. As a boss, it is *your* responsibility to find out what tools your people require and then make sure you provide them.

Chew on this

What tools help you do your own job better?

How frequently do you ask your staff members (or spouse, or children) what tools they need to be productive?

Reminders—How to put the right tools in your people's hands

- Across all sectors, be sure to provide:
  A great product
  Pleasant interactions with personnel
  Easy and clear procedures
- Make sure employees have the right tools and the right information to excel.
- Know when to call for help—and who the right person to call is!
- Look for simple solutions, like buying purple plastic paper clips.
- To figure out what your people need, just ask.
- Focus on setting up your people for success, not failure.

Remember—Making sure the right tools are in place enhances productivity.

LESSON 7

DO THE RIGHT THING WITH THE RIGHT SPIRIT

Work Like a Dog with the Right Spirit

Life improved for me when I started to behave more like Rudder, and I wish more people behaved like her, too. Why? Because Rudder responds cheerfully and enthusiastically to any activity. She bounds to greet me at every opportunity. She wags with her whole body when I announce we're going for a walk. She shows me she's excited to go *anywhere*, even to the vet's office, and makes me believe I'm the most important person in the universe.

Here's how to adopt a dog's spirit in the workplace:

- Work with enthusiasm.
- Support the boss's ideas.
- Focus attentively.

Work with enthusiasm—Let's face it, on some days (especially Mondays), your enthusiasm for work can be downright low. Fueled by copious cups of coffee and grumbling all the way, you contemplate calling in sick with ideas of going to the beach, shopping, sleeping, or even getting household chores done.

But if you brought a dog's enthusiasm to work, you'd start the day feeling cheerful and smiling. You'd trust it would be full of challenges, yet you'd feel confident knowing you can handle whatever happens. You'd worry less about the bad things that might happen. Feeling grateful that you're healthy enough to work, you'd happily muster up lots of zeal for the day's activities.

Support the boss's ideas—Whether you're a manager, supervisor, or lower in the ranks, has your boss ever come up with a seemingly brainless, time-consuming idea? ("No, not my boss," you say as you roll your eyes.) Well, yes, sometimes. Dog owners, too.

My dogs show enthusiastic support all the time. Sure, Rudder and Dolly may think it's ridiculous to lock up the house, get into the car, and drive fifteen minutes for a Starbucks coffee when I have a coffee maker at home. They nevertheless eagerly race to the car, leap into the seats, and stick their heads out the window.

Most bosses probably don't expect you to show that kind of exuberance, but consider how your work life would improve if you applied open-mindedness and excitement in response to your boss's ideas.

꙳꙳

You Never Know Where Great Ideas Come From

Back in the 1990s, my boss's wife came up with an idea that I thought was ridiculous. (And, yes, it is bad enough when the boss gets a stupid idea, but getting told how to do your job from the boss's *spouse*?) Regardless of its source, I deemed it a stupid idea.

I was wrong.

She suggested starting a free drop-in childcare center at the military medical facility, rightly noting that parents miss medical appointments because of lack of child care. I grumbled about having to implement the program in addition to everything else on my plate. But in retrospect, it was a great idea. Kids were happy, parents were happy, and the costs and management (once I stopped rolling my eyes) turned out to be reasonable.

Humor the boss sometimes. He or she may be right!

છ્ન્જ

Focus attentively—Sometimes when others talk or you're trapped in another endless meeting, are you listening as attentively as you could? Perhaps you're thinking about what you'll say when it's *your* turn, or you're pondering the growing pile of work on your desk. Not great focus.

My dog, however, excels at having great focus. When Dolly lies down, her eyes are locked on me. When I move around the room, she turns her head to follow my movements. She looks at me directly and waits for me to give her attention. When I get up to go into another room, even if it is just to move clothes from the washer into the dryer, she follows me to the garage, the closet, and of course the kitchen, her eyes always on me. Wouldn't it be great if our employees possessed such focus?

Maybe we can do a better job of focusing our attention in the workplace. We can listen completely to what people say. We can concentrate on the issue at hand instead of allowing stray thoughts to impede our work. We can strive to give other people the full attention my dog gives me.

When I feel sluggish, drowsy, or unmotivated, I think of my dog. If people exhibited the enthusiasm, support, and focus dogs have, they'd be unstoppable.

Respect a Variety of Perspectives

Do human beings always see eye to eye? No. Do your people always understand your perspective in your role as leader? No, they don't—especially if you work in an office with people who are used to operating independently. They may not be thrilled to buy into your vision.

As a leader, your job is to competently communicate as much good information as effectively as possible so people understand the requirements. Some will take your direction and say, "Okay, boss. Got it." Others will say, "But boss, I need more information. Why are you changing to this different form? Why do we have to do this differently?" No doubt you know this firsthand: Change often meets resistance.

In addition, leading different generational groups takes extra effort, unique skills, and a special approach. Every generation contributes its own values, experiences, and assets. It takes patience to understand their skills and motivations to maximize the value of each generation's contributions.

Fielding stereotypical comments about various generations is common, of course, when I'm talking to another group. Leaders make a practice of challenging stereotypes. For one group you might ask, "Where is this company going to be in twenty years?" For another group you query, "How do you think this company got where it is today?" Their answers shed light on perspectives that are important to know.

Candid communication between generations often results in a change in perspectives. For example, a military veteran might give someone from a younger generation a new perspective on wars today; a more mature worker might better appreciate the nuances of a computer marketing program after talking with a student about social marketing and networking. (Even my mom is on Facebook!)

Different perspectives are critical to success. If everyone thought and acted like everyone else, fewer ideas would emerge. Look around and ask, "What might you learn from each other?" Take advantage of the talents and experiences of others.

Chew on this

What prevents your people from doing the right thing with the right spirit? How can you encourage their enthusiasm?

What makes leading different generations particularly challenging? What makes having them in your organization an asset?

What will your company look like in twenty years and who will lead it?

Reminders—How to do the right thing in the right spirit

- Communicate fully and competently so that your people understand the direction you want them to take.
- Be enthusiastic, supportive, and focused— like canine companions are!
- Attempt to understand the differing perspectives from all generations.

Remember—Leaders communicate their visions with clarity and work every day with a spirit of enthusiasm, support, and focus!

LESSON 8

DO THE RIGHT THING AT THE RIGHT TIME

Intentional Acts of Kindness

Do you spend much time in airports? I recently observed random acts of genuine concern and kindness in several airports in various parts of the country. Here are a few of them:

- A man helped a woman in her thirties get checked in at the ticket counter. She was flying for the first time, and she didn't know how to check in her bags.
- In the security area, people cheerfully stood aside to allow two frenzied, late, and stressed airline workers get to their plane.
- On a completely booked flight, three people helped reorganize the overhead bin to accommodate the bags of the three late arrivals.
- People applauded when uniformed military personnel boarded the plane.
- At baggage claim, two gentlemen lifted the bags of three others who had trouble lifting them off the carousel.
- People held elevator doors for others who struggled with multiple bags.

- A mature couple offered to watch the luggage of a woman with a baby needing attention.
- A woman got a bottle of water for another woman confined to a wheelchair.

Essentially, the people I observed demonstrated considerate, empathetic, and polite actions. They did the right things at the right times.

When It's Not Easy

A few years ago, I moved from Hawaii to Maryland. Perfect Hawaii weather year-round had eliminated the necessity for air conditioning or heat in our home, so I wasn't accustomed to what could go wrong.

In Maryland, I lived in a rented (military owned) townhouse with my puppy, Dolly. One Sunday night, I was upstairs reading when she came bounding up the steps, my little cute puppy with the little blue eyes and wavy brown hair.

"Rarr. Woof."

"Do you have to go outside, Dolly?" I asked.

"Rarr. Woof!"

"Are you hungry?"

"Rarr, woof!" she insisted.

I looked at her in joking alarm. "Timmy's in the well?"

I went trotting downstairs and immediately saw the problem. Her dog bed was floating in my living room. Dolly took a leap from the third stair (because the first two were covered with water) and landed on the dog bed, which promptly skidded out from under her. She fell into the water, splashing happily. Then she looked up at me with glee and said, "Mom! You're the greatest ever! Nobody else has a swimming pool *in* the house!" It was February, it was ten degrees outside, and the water pipe in the ceiling had burst.

If you've ever been curious about what the inside of a ceiling looks like, I found out. Broken water pipes from the ceiling were now on my floor, and flooding the main level of the house. At a pressure of forty pounds per square inch (pressure I never enjoyed in the shower there), the water was soaking my belongings, the carpet, and the walls.

My calls to anybody with an emergency number— local utilities, fire department, and police department— resulted in verbal shrugs. "Sorry. It's not my jurisdiction. We can't handle that." I finally got the military housing call center with this polite response: "I'm sorry, ma'am. It's nine-thirty at night. We can have somebody there at seven in the morning to shut off your water for you."

This certainly wasn't the right thing at the right time. I then responded in my calmest voice, "Ma'am, I don't think you understand my situation. I have the equivalent of a fire hydrant shooting water into my ceiling, and that water is now most inconveniently cascading onto the floor." She again repeated, "I'm sorry, ma'am. I'm in Connecticut. What do you want me to do?"

I didn't exactly know what I wanted her to do, but I did know she wasn't providing the right answer for me. About then, my neighbor, who played football, came over after seeing water seep into his house. "I think I know where the water shutoff valve is!" he shouted like a superhero, and then busted down a locked door to get to it. Thank goodness he did the right thing before the wrong thing got worse!

The Four P's

People make mistakes, especially during tough times, yet how they handle these mistakes is critical, which is why businesses should plan for how to solve problems before they arise. I suggest an approach I call the "Four P's":

- **P**op the blister.
- Make a **P**lan of action.
- Put a **P**rocedure in place so everyone knows what to do.
- **P**olish the procedure to try to reduce systematic errors.

Sometimes people avoid solving problems because they're afraid they will be criticized for:

- Creating the problem.
- Not solving the problem on their own.
- Not placating the customer.
- Involving the boss.

When employees are not actively encouraged to find and solve problems, these problems get ignored or, worse, hidden. The longer a problem stews, the worse it usually gets.

So I suggest you find a way to **P**op the blister (ascertain the problem), then develop a **P**lan (to resolve the problem), and set up a **P**rocedure or system to fix whatever caused the problem in the first place. That prevents a repeat of the problem. Then **P**olish the procedure by reevaluating the system and the process to determine how to improve efficiency and reduce errors overall. Many people feel stuck in a system that creates and compounds mistakes because the processes are antiquated, the customer needs have changed, or the outcome is no longer valuable.

ॐॐ
The Four P's in Action

I was lucky to work at the Navy's Pacific personnel and payroll support detachment. We were responsible for 17,000 people, from California to the Middle East, handling everything travel or pay-related for the Pacific Ocean Area of Responsibility (AOR). Our front-line customer service team often fixed problems that started 7,000 miles away. I told my staff, "Some people come in or call in, and they're mad. I don't believe you're getting paid enough to listen to somebody be ugly to you, but you are responsible for solving their problems."

We developed a way to deal with rude people. Every staff person had some of my business cards at their desks. When a customer got obnoxious, I never took it as the staff's failure to handle or diffuse the problem; my staff person simply needed support from me. Sometimes people just want to complain to the boss. So I told them to say, "You know, I think you might like to talk to my supervisor. Let's walk into her office." When one of my people walked into my office with my business card in hand and said, "I'd like to introduce you to Lynn," I always knew that "Lynn" wasn't a happy customer.

After welcoming Lynn, I **P**opped the blister to get to the root of the problem and said, "Tell me everything that has gone wrong today and where this all started." I listened and then suggested, "Let's set up a **P**lan to make it right. I guarantee that I'll call you within twenty-four hours and tell you exactly how we'll make it right. Not only that, but I'll call your boss and apologize for your loss of productivity because you're not at work."

Doing the right thing at the right time meant providing Lynn with a **P**lan of action to fix her problem—one that was right for her—then setting up a **P**rocedure to correct the issue while making sure both Lynn and her boss knew exactly when and how the problem would be solved. I also gave both of them my personal cell phone number. Then we **P**olished the procedure by determining where the root cause of the problem lay, and tried to solve any future issues before they developed into a situation like Lynn's.

પ્≈∽

Problems are like broccoli in a glass of milk; they don't hide well. Somebody finds out eventually. That's why I prefer to get the problem out in the open and get it handled properly. Having the right intentions are grand, but if the timing is not right or if the situation isn't resolved, more problems will pop. And who needs more problems?

As leaders, it's our responsibility to make sure the right thing gets done at the right time, so we don't end up with broccoli trying to hide in our glass of milk.

Give Rewards to Encourage the Right Thing at the Right Time

Rudder consistently does what I ask. When I say "sit" and hold the treat above her nose, her back end goes down, her face goes up, and she sits. I started training her when she was a seven-week-old puppy. After a few of these exercises, she realized what the word "sit" meant. During the training phase, if I asked her to sit, and she sat right away, she got a treat. If she didn't, I helped her get into a sitting position and directly told her that what she was doing was a "sit." In that case, she got no treat. We repeated this process until her sitting response became a reliable event. Today, I can always depend on her to sit whenever I ask.

Imagine how fast Rudder learned that she gets treats when she does The right thing at the right time.

Similarly, when I was training her to walk nicely on a leash, I'd dangle a treat near her nose and we'd take a few steps. We'd stop, and I asked her to sit, again with the treat held slightly above her nose. If she sat down, she earned another treat. Rudder figured this process out quickly: she gets treats for walking when I walk and for stopping when I stop. Because she wants the treat, she watches me to see what I am doing so that she can do that, too. When we go out, she pays attention to my behavior because I might have that treat for her when she responds at the right time. And because she is now trained, she still gives me the behavior I want, even if I don't give her a treat every time.

"Thank you" as a reward—Not only is it important to do the right thing at the right time, it's also critical to thank your employees at the right time. Lesson One was all about rewarding good behavior, but it bears repeating here because appropriate timing is as important as displaying the right kind of reward. You might dismiss this idea with, "I already do a great job of recognizing my employees." Maybe you already convey to employees that they are valued, important, and appreciated. But if you find that someone has placed this book on your desk or in your mailbox as a strong hint, maybe you aren't doing quite as well as you think you are.

Positive feedback works. People like to be sincerely appreciated, especially by their supervisors. As discussed in Lesson One, employees won't complain about receiving too much positive reinforcement. But employers often overlook the necessity of *strengthening the intrinsic motivation* in the workplace.

Intrinsic means *it comes from within*. It's the drive or ambition that stems from within oneself. Ideally, all of your people are self-starters who work hard because they love their jobs. In a perfect world, all employees would be intrinsically motivated. *Extrinsic motivation* derives from other sources. (Like you.)

How do you, as a boss, reward employees? A good rule—the golden rule—is to treat them as you want your boss to treat you. However, as discussed in Lesson One, what resonates for one employee may not work with another. The important thing is to make sure employees realize they are valued.

Chew on this

How can you turn a mistake into an opportunity in the right time frame?

How can you apply the Four P's in your environment?

How will you display your appreciation to those you work with?

Reminders—*How to ensure your intentions and timing are right for solving problems*

- Have confidence that you can handle mistakes easily with respect, not blame.
- Implement the Four P's:
- **P**op the blister and get to the root of the problem.
- Make a **P**lan to set the problem situation right.
- Have a **P**rocedure so people know what to do.
- **P**olish the process so mistakes are not repeated.
- Show your employees you appreciate them with "treats" given at the right time.

Remember—*Leaders respond appropriately and immediately to problems. Fix the problems, not the blame.*

LESSON 9
SERVE WITH A CHEERFUL HEART

Wake Up and Fake It

My dog Rudder was a show dog.

The dog show world is fun and exciting, but it is also competitive. People spend a lot of money showing their dogs. Many people ship their dogs to professional dog handlers to make the dog show circuits in the hopes of securing a championship title. Clearly, they take dog shows very seriously.

But we are not those people. We did not take our dog shows seriously. We entered the shows because we promised Trudi we would, and because Rudder's whole litter did the dog show adventure together.

We started showing our dogs when they were only six months old. Do you know what the puppy class of a dog show looks like? Mostly chaos. Lots of dogs jumping, leaping, grabbing at the leash and barking. It is hilarious. Yes, technically, we were competing against each other. We swapped dogs and took each other's dogs into the ring in an effort to get them to calm down. It didn't work. Winning wasn't our big concern; having trained dogs that were healthy and having fun was the goal.

Some dogs really like being show dogs, but Rudder just didn't care. She willingly did what I asked because I asked her to do it, but she plainly thought the idea of trotting in a ring behind a Great Dane and in front of the Doberman was a little stupid. I know this because she gave me the "Mom, this stupid" look. But she did it.

Rudder does what I ask happily, even when she would rather be doing other activities. Can we get people to do that—serve with the right spirit regardless of the activity or environment?

Walter Williams, one of my favorite economists, says, "You don't have to love your neighbors. Just serve them."

Similarly, you don't have to come into work happy every day, but if you work with customers, you *do* have to at least *pretend* to be happy at your job every day. Sometimes life is hard. You get that late-night phone call, or you have problems with your teenager, your parents, or your toddler. You're tired, over-committed, and over-whelmed by a multitude of challenges.

Still, serving with a cheerful heart is extremely important because others are affected by your mood, responses, and actions. So if you don't have the right spirit on a given day, fake it. (I think putting on lipstick helps a lot—though maybe not so much for men.) Additionally, we become our thoughts and actions. If we pretend to be cheerful, we eventually become more cheerful.

Exactly what it means to serve with a cheerful heart can differ based on geography. I grew up in the southern U.S. where customers go into local roadside diners and are greeted as "sweetheart," "honey," and "baby." Your age or gender doesn't matter. You can sit in a red vinyl booth and drink coffee all morning, and the wait staff cheerfully keeps refilling your cup while calling you "darlin'" and "sugah" throughout the entire visit. (One obvious advantage to this system is that we don't have to worry about remembering too many names.)

How different was my experience in a deli in New York City. All I wanted was a bagel and some coffee, but I was greeted with a loud, "*What do you want?*" I managed to say, 'Uhm, nothing." I got out of line and went to the back, this time prepared to answer his gruff question.

I realized the man behind the deli counter had a completely different perspective from mine. While *I* didn't perceive he was serving bagels and coffee with a cheerful heart, *he* thought he was. Plus his demeanor was completely aligned with the crowded deli culture of New York.

See how other people's cheerful hearts may be different from yours?

ॐ ॐ

"Have To" or "Get To"

My friend, Tim Sanders, wrote a book called *Love Is The Killer App*. In it, he coaches readers on how to change their mindsets. His advice? To get through a day, don't say, "I have to pick up the kids. I have to take them to soccer practice. I have to wash the dog. I have to get dinner ready." Instead, change "have to" to "get to." Say, "I get to take the kids to school. I get to pick up the family at the airport. I get to make dinner for my loved ones."

For example, I *get* to pick up the doggy deposits in the yard.

This approach provides a completely different way of looking at the universe and gives a sense of abundance and gratitude, not duty. "I get to be with you today" feels so much better than "I have to."

My advice? Take on happier ways of viewing the world and you'll make leadership enjoyable for yourself and those around you.

෯෴

How a Dog Models the Right Spirit

What might happen if you adopted doggy behaviors in the spirit of being happy at work? Metaphorically speaking, you would:

- Chase the squirrels.
- Leap exuberantly into the water.
- Adopt a dog's "get to" attitude.

Chase the squirrels—My dogs shoot out of the house like rockets to chase the squirrels that have the audacity to frolic on *their* grass. They race toward the tree and bark at the squirrels, who indignantly bark back at them. Few dogs ever actually *catch* the squirrels. (Dolly did once, and it was a disaster, particularly for the unfortunate squirrel. But that's another story.) The point is: Lack of success doesn't stop the dogs from making the effort.

How often in business do you hold back from chasing the next level because the chase takes effort? Advancement takes effort; staying current in your field requires effort; having a great attitude takes effort.

You may not need to chase *all* the latest information or technologies, but you're wise to stay current in your area of specialization. Read trade journals, newsletters, and the latest news of your company and your industry. Apply focus to keeping up with information. Even knowing what's the right information to chase takes effort. Can you learn to enjoy the chase itself?

Leap exuberantly into the water (but know where the stairs are)—My older dog, Rudder, loves water and leaps into the swimming pool with reckless abandon to chase a ball, catch a Frisbee, or play with kids.

When she was a puppy, however, my breeder Trudi impressed on me the importance of teaching Rudder how to get *out* of a pool or any body of water. Even the most natural swimming dogs, such as Labradors, Newfoundlands, or retrievers often drown—not because they don't know how to swim, but because they don't know how to get out of the pool! They exhaust themselves trying. It's vitally important that the dogs find the pool steps so they can get out on their own.

To train Rudder, I put her on the pool's top two stairs and kept repeating, "Stairs, stairs, stairs." As she was preparing to get out, I guided her to the stairs, pointed, and repeated the word again. Then I repeated the same lesson in the ocean, labeling the beach access as "stairs." I applied the same lesson to the exiting from different pools.

Within weeks, whenever I pointed and said "stairs" and pointed, she recognized that location as a place to safely enter and exit the water and headed confidently in that direction. These lessons increased both her confidence and mine. Now I can take her anywhere. I know when I say "stairs" that she'll find her way out of the water.

When you take risks and "jump in the pool," make sure you know you have a safe out. Taking risks can be necessary, exhilarating, and even profitable, but know where to turn when it's time to move on. Your "stairs" might be the boss who lets you try out new ideas, friends who help you develop entrepreneurial thoughts, or family members who support your dreams. Find the stairs—a safe place to take a break and reassess your plans and goals.

Adopt a dog's "get to" attitude—Because dogs throw everything into their daily activities, they give us a great career lesson. How many times do we drag ourselves to work? Switch to some of that doggy enthusiasm! Wake yourself up the way the dog does. Have a stretch, take a short walk outside, have breakfast, and adopt the dog's attitude: *Today, this moment, right now, is the best day ever! Wag! Wag! Wag!*

Treat your workplace as the most fun, best place to be at that moment. (You're going to be there anyway, so might as well enjoy your time.) Work with the same exuberance and crazy joy that your dog shows when you suggest going for a w-a-l-k. When you start to slump at work, remember to throw yourself into your day. Motivational speakers might say this is simply a different way to change your attitude, and I might agree, but I prefer to think of it as a "doggy solution" to an attitude problem.

Who knows? Activity that resembles living like a dog might give you just the boost you need!

The Law of the Garbage Truck

How often do you allow other people's nonsense to change your mood? Do you let a bad driver, a rude waiter, a curt employee, or an insensitive coworker ruin your day? Unless you're invincible, for an instant you might let such a person put you in a bad mood. The mark of successful people is how quickly they get their focus back to what's important.

A friend relayed this story about a garbage truck He heard it in the back of a New York City taxi on the way to Grand Central Station. The taxi was in the right lane when a black car suddenly jumped out of a parking space right in front of it. The taxi driver slammed on his brakes, swerved, and barely missed crashing into the other car's back end.

The driver of the black car—the guy who almost caused a big accident—whipped his head around and started yelling profanities. The taxi driver simply smiled and waved at the guy. He was downright *friendly.* So my friend asked, "Why did you do that? This guy almost ruined your car and could have killed us!" The taxi driver responded with The Law of the Garbage Truck.

"Many people are like garbage trucks," he said philosophically. "They run around full of garbage—frustration, anger, and disappointment. When their garbage piles up, they need a place to dump it. If you let them, they'll dump it on you.

"When someone wants to dump on you, don't take it personally. Smile, wave, wish them well, and move on. You'll be happy you did."

The Law of the Garbage Truck—how often do you let Garbage Trucks run right over you? And how often do you accept their garbage and spread it to others at work, at home, or on the streets?

The day I heard that story, I thought, "I'm not going to accept garbage anymore," and I began to see Garbage Trucks everywhere

I see the garbage loads people carry. I see them coming to drop it off on me. And like the taxi driver, I don't take it personally. I try to smile, wave, wish them well, and move on. How therapeutic!

Life gives us a finite but unpredictable number of minutes. That doesn't leave time to feel wronged by Garbage Trucks. Why wake up in the morning with regrets? Instead, love the people who treat you well and be kind to those who don't.

The Importance of Community

The "Responsibility Revolution" is a term coined by Tim Sanders (*Saving the World at Work*) to describe the new approach to social ownership of responsibility. Feeling rich in the belief that we live in a world of plenty (a very doggy philosophy), these revolutionaries are making a point to contribute to the greater good. They're volunteering, reaching out, and using their time and money to leverage social and corporate change. It's the way of the future.

Did you know the recession of 2008-2009 sparked an increase, not a decrease, in volunteerism? You would think that people who were fearful about their futures would devote *more* time to developing their own human capital and not worry about others around them. That didn't prove to be true. People who were volunteers before still volunteered, and people who were suddenly without a full-time job volunteered because:

- They needed something to do.
- They wanted to contribute something useful.
- They knew volunteering could create possibilities for finding full-time jobs.

People discovered that their communities were more important to them than ever. They joined groups such as the Red Cross and other clubs and societies, Not for monetary gain, but for a spirit of community greater than they had before.

This increase in volunteerism showed that when times get tough, people need each other more. Thank you to everyone who volunteers in schools, churches, hospitals, community centers, Girl Scouts, Little League, senior centers, welcome centers, airports, and of course, those therapy dog teams. They routinely make cheer-up visits to senior centers, retirement homes, inner-city children centers, hospice units, homeless shelters, and other places where people need a hand.

కeత

A Big Cheer for Volunteers

Surprisingly, tough economic times have increased the level of volunteerism in America. At the USO in Denver, Colorado, for example, engineers, doctors, teachers, and many others make coffee and sandwiches for military service members and their families. Many of the volunteers were in the military themselves, were part of a military family, had kids in the military, or took advantage of the USO when they were on active duty. They want to help others. Even though the Denver USO doesn't advertise for volunteers, it has a waiting list of 160 people (more than a year long) signed up to be one of the volunteers. Wow! That's intrinsic motivation.

At Memorial Hospital in Colorado Springs, volunteers come from all sectors and simply want to help.

Amazing! The motivation of these volunteers to pick up shifts, fill in for others, deliver dinners, and be a comforting shoulder in times of crisis is nothing short of awe-inspiring.

Volunteers tend to serve with a cheerful heart because they make the decision to show up. And every time they start a shift, they reaffirm their commitment to the good of the organization.

ふぺ

Great volunteers approach their voluntary jobs with the same level of commitment as paid staff. Many times, they are *more* committed. Why? Because they truly want to be part of a group of people who are making a difference. They are fully committed to the goals of the project or organization, and when they arrive, they are excited to participate.

The difference is the attitude they bring with them. The want to serve and they serve with a cheerful heart. Are all volunteers fabulous? Well, honestly, no. Some just show up for the cookies…but it's the GREAT ones organizations want to hang on to forever.

Chew on this

How do you handle the Garbage Trucks in your life in a positive way?

What activities do you "get" to do every day?

Reminders—How to serve with a cheerful heart

- Approach both customers and employees with a cheerful heart.
- Think of all the things you have to do, then replace the word "have" with "get."
- Don't let the Garbage Trucks dump on you.
- Volunteer. Become part of a bigger community.

Remember—If you didn't wake up with a great attitude, fake it. Don't be a Garbage Truck to others.

LESSON 10
DON'T JERK THE LEASH

Walking Your Dog Takes Practice

Many humans believe that getting a dog to walk nicely on a leash is as simple as attaching a rope to a collar. Actually persuading a dog to walk politely next to you on your left side while not dragging you, pulling you, or otherwise engaging in sled-dog behavior takes training, practice, and persistence. It's simply not in the dog's nature to walk placidly next to you when:

- You walk too slowly.
- There are squirrels to chase! And bunnies! And cars!
- There are a myriad of scents to smell, including dead stuff to sniff on the other side of the street.

With an unlimited number of distractions, walking calmly on a leash takes practice. When dog owners are confronted by another dog, car, or squirrel, they panic, jerk the leash, and forcefully cause unwanted consequences.

If you're the one jerking the leash, you may be operating from a place of fear. Don't do it. You'll make the problem worse. Having a "leash" is helpful. Most people know what the perimeters are, but the leash also must be long enough to let people do their jobs and not feel jerked around.

An Inconvenience or a Problem?

I got a phone call a few years ago that changed my world. I learned from the doctor that my husband had an aggressive and evil form of cancer. I was less than a year away From retiring from the military with a job at the local university. My husband loved his job in Hawaii and we loved living there. The house, the pool, the dogs—we had it all. I certainly didn't worry about frozen ceiling pipes breaking.

Only fifty-five days after his diagnosis, my husband passed.

That awful time crashed my world. But it also taught me the biggest lesson of all—the life-changing clarity on the difference between a problem and an inconvenience.

Make Time for the Important Things

Watching people in airports provides an excellent study in human behavior—and comic relief—as I watch travelers juggle their possessions. Everything important to them when they travel is contained within a few precious pieces of luggage, which they then turn over to perfect strangers for handling, sorting, and inspecting.

A Transportation Security Administration employee told me about a woman who was particularly irate at the thought of losing her shampoo and conditioner at the security checkpoint. She threw her clothes on the ground and shouted at the TSA employee. I should mention that these items were of the complimentary kind found in high-end hotels. Yep, that's right. The woman was mad because TSA was confiscating the little bottles she had taken from her hotel that morning. She wasn't embarrassed, or chagrined, or even disturbed that she didn't know the travel rules. She felt she was being wronged. She was a Garbage Truck.

Not everyone travels enough to know all the rules. So, yes, when the rules change, it's easy to feel unprepared and upset when you lose your possessions to a trash can.

If you travel often, you have horror stories, right? What are some of your travel worries? Getting stuck or rerouted at the last minute? Missing a connection? Not having space for your luggage? Lost luggage? Lost ticket? Lost in an airport?

But what should you really be concerned about? Yep, the plane! Will it fall out of the sky? By getting preoccupied by the little things, sometimes we forget the big ones.

Today when an airline attendant says, "Mary, you get the middle seat between the professional wrestler and the lady holding an infant," I say, "Cool." It's a temporary inconvenience, not a real problem.

Living life takes management, too. Kids need to get to school, dogs need to be fed, cars need gas, bills need to be paid, and you need to go to work. Life doesn't stop just because priorities change. Your challenge is making time for the *important* things while managing the *urgent* things, too.

Effective leaders differentiate between problems and inconveniences—and make sure our people understand the differences as well.

Blessings Abound

During the recession of 2009, I became close with several families who panicked when the father or the mother lost a job. In the process of coping and setting priorities, they learned two important things:

1. They could do without the second salary they thought they needed, and
2. Some weren't making all that much extra when they considered the additional taxes, work clothes required, need for another vehicle and gas, child care, and other job-related costs.

In effect, that second job wasn't improving their standard of living at all.

Because of the slow economy, job-loss disasters have turned into blessings for some people. Parents suddenly had more time to spend with their children, more time to enjoy their homes, and more time to be involved in their children's and each others' lives.

As an economist, it pains me to say this, but sometimes it pays *not* to be paid for your labor. During the recession, volunteerism increased as people with free time used it to help change their communities. They didn't let life jerk them around. Instead, they transformed difficult situations into blessings for themselves and for others.

How great is that?

Chew on this

Are you confusing an inconvenience with a real problem?

What are you dealing with that could be considered just an inconvenience rather than a problem?

Reminders—How to keep your priorities in perspective

- Take time to evaluate what's most important in your life.
- Be available for employees and family; they need you most during tough times.
- Calmly figure out your strategic plan of action and turn problems into blessings.
- Avoid overreacting when events don't turn out exactly as you'd planned. They seldom do.

Remember—As a leader, don't operate from fear and jerk others around.

CONCLUSION
WALK THE TALK

Walking Your Talk

The Hawaiian word "kina'ole" means *to do the right thing, at the right time, to the right person, with the right spirit, every time.* That is the key to successful living today, tomorrow, and always.

After reading through all ten lessons, I hope these realizations stay with you:

1. All these lessons learned from dogs can apply to bosses, coworkers, employees, friends, even spouses, children, and, of course, dogs (not so much on cats; I have no idea what works with cats).

2. You can share these lessons and pay it forward. People always remember those who cared enough to do so. Ultimately, your number one mission is to help other people succeed.

Most of all, remember that good leaders foster healthy, connected relationships that model, inspire, challenge, enable, and encourage. They know how to collaborate and build trust because they act with integrity; they're committed to the success of their organization and its people; and they're honest, focused, positive, loving, and loyal.

They "walk their talk."

Sounds like a really good dog, doesn't it?

About the Author

Mary Kelly, PhD, is the CEO of Productive Leaders, a consulting firm specializing in professional keynote speaking and business training in leadership, productivity, communications, and management. Dr. Kelly graduated from the U.S. Naval Academy and spent 21 on active duty in the Navy, retiring as a commander. She taught at both the Naval Academy in Annapolis, Maryland and the Air Force Academy in Colorado Springs, Colorado.

As a change agent, she has successfully worked with educational groups, military organizations, non-profits, and Fortune 500 companies for more than twenty years. She specializes in helping leaders obtain desired behaviors from others and resolving common misunderstandings in the workplace for greater productivity and higher morale.

An active volunteer, Dr. Kelly enjoys visiting nursing homes, shelters, and hospitals with her two dogs, Rudder and Dolly.

Resources

Adams, Henry. *Collected Works of Henry Adams.* New York: Library of America, 1983.

Buckingham, Marcus. *The One Thing We Need to Know.* New York: Free Press, 2005.

———. *First, Break All the Rules.* New York: Free Press, 2005.

Covey, Stephen R. *The 8th Habit.* FranklinCovey, 2004.

Goldsmith, Marshall. *Mojo: How to Get It, How to Keep It, How to Get It Back If You Lose It.* New York: Hyperion, 2010.

Maxwell, John C. *The 21 Indispensable Qualities of a Leader.* Nashville, Tenn.: Thomas Nelson, 2007.

———. *Everyone Communicates, Few Connect.* Nashville, Tenn.: Thomas Nelson, 2010.

Sanders, Tim. *Love Is the Killer App.* New York: Random House, 2002.

———. *Saving the World at Work.* New York: Crown Business, 2008.

Smith, Adam. *An Inquiry into the Nature and Causes of the Wealth of Nations.* (First published 1776; available from Modern Library and other publishers.)

Quick Order Form

Master Your World 10 Dog-Inspired Leadership Lessons to Improve Productivity, Profits and Communication

Four ways to order this book:
1. Telephone: Call Productive Leaders at 719-357-7360 with credit card.
2. Mail: Clip or copy and mail this form to: Kaimana Publishing, P.O. Box 461350, Denver, CO 80246
3. Email: **Mary@ProductiveLeaders.com**
4. Go to www.Amazon.com

Payment: Make checks payable in U.S. dollars to Mary Kelly and mail to:
Kaimana Publishing
P.O. Box 461350
Denver, CO 80246

Please send more FREE information on:
Speaking/Seminars   Consulting   A d d me to newsletter list Other books

Name: _____
Address: _____
City: _____ State: _____ Zip: _____

Telephone: _____
Email: _____

Pricing: $19.95 per book, plus $2.75 shipping and handling for first book ordered. For each additional book, add $1.50 shipping/handling. Please call for a bulk rate for over 100 copies.

Quantity	Item	Cost	Amount Due
_____	*Master Your World*	$19.95	_____
Shipping/Handling 1st copy		$2.75	_____
Shipping/Handling __ copies @$1.50		_____	_____
TOTAL			_____

Delivery in U.S.: Books will be mailed via Priority Mail (U.S. Postal Service).

International: $9.00 for shipping/handling for first book; $5.00 for each additional.